Finance for Non-Financiers 4

Finance for Non-Financiers 4

Special Finances

José Saul Velásquez Restrepo

Copyright © 2010 by José Saul Velásquez Restrepo.

Número de Control de la Biblioteca del Congreso de EE. UU.: 2010940020
ISBN: Hardcover 978-1-6176-4279-1
Softcover 978-1-6176-4281-4
Ebook 978-1-6176-4280-7

All rights reserved. No part of this book may be reproduced or transmitted in any form or by any means, electronic or mechanical, including photocopying, recording, or by any information storage and retrieval system, without permission in writing from the copyright owner.

The information, ideas, and suggestions in this book are not intended to render professional advice. Before following any suggestions contained in this book, you should consult your personal accountant or other financial advisor. Neither the author nor the publisher shall be liable or responsible for any loss or damage allegedly arising as a consequence of your use or application of any information or suggestions in this book.

This book was printed in the United States of America.

Para pedidos de copias adicionales de este libro, por favor contacte con:
Palibrio
1663 Liberty Drive
Suite 200
Bloomington, IN 47403
Llamadas desde los EE.UU. 877.407.5847
Llamadas internacionales +1.812.671.9757
Fax: +1.812.355.1576
ventas@palibrio.com

Contents

Chapter 1: How To Quality A Country For Practical Applications 9

Chapter 2: Intellectual Capital 15

Chapter 3: Accounting And Companies Of Century XXI 20

Chapter 4: Application Of The Statistics To The Finances 25

Chapter 5: Happiness And Productivity 34

Chapter 6: Approaches To Personal Quality 42

Chapter 7: Internationalization And Globalization 52

Chapter 8: How To Make A Competitive Enterprise 58

Chapter 9: Reflections On Leadership 69

Chapter 10: Making A Decision Correctly 77

Chapter 11: The Generation Of Value And The Human Resource 82

Chapter 12: Budgets, Simple Norms And Continuous Improvement 88

Introduction

I wrote these issues with the aim to make it easier which apparently is too difficult and above all, with the desire to contribute to the formation of a theory totally applicable in real life. This is a description available to everyone, though this could hardly be called a lack of depth in any of the items, which makes the text highly recommended for non-financial executives.

The approach is very practical; based on a great deal of evidence to avoid any situation that may arise in the business world and apply personal finances.

The papers are presented according to the recommended order of learning and practical exercises are made in Excel.

It is an effort that I have enthusiastically encouraged by many friends, who have helped me to mature and clarify concepts. There are so many that fail to list them and so I refrain from doing so to avoid being unfair by omitting any name oblivion unintentional. In all, my sincere thanks, on behalf of those who can draw some profit from this book.

josavere

Chapter 1

HOW TO QUALITY A COUNTRY FOR PRACTICAL APPLICATIONS

1. INTRODUCTION

There are a great quantity of statistics dispersed, depending of the sources that consult, doing difficult the possibility to emit a judgment.

As far as possible—because the model is debatable—present a yardstick that allows comparing quantitatively the standard living of countries in order to provide useful comparisons and targets to overcome.

2. VARIABLES TO USE

The variables to use depend of the practice application of the model; of course one subject is the classification of the countries speaking of soccer and other of productivity; the important is to make a correct selection for the specific use and the correct indicators. The example of the use of the model is related with the quality of live in different countries-that are important for the situation in study—the more universal and feasible for made the compare are the following:

A. CALORIES / DAY / INHABITANT: indicate the average of calories that the inhabitants consume. It is an **utmost** representative indicator; answer the more elementary human needs. According to concept of experts' in the theme, the human need around **2,500** calories day. The excess is worrying because generates various types of diseases; the deficit generates malnutrition. The maximum score is granted to the calories need/day.

B. INFANTILE MORTALITY: the children represent the bigger expression of love, so that it is easy to deduct the importance from his care and the level of effort for his growth and development. The relation with the level of quality of life is inversely proportional.

C. PER-CAPITA INCOME: measure the average of entrance per capita at a country. Money is extremely important to satisfy human basic needs, prerequisite to survive and pass to superior level (social and spiritual). His behavior is directly proportional at the same level as quality of life.

D. LEVEL OF ILLITERACY: the nutrition is base for human development. The education follows in importance in order to better quality of life, dialing difference with animals. The social intelligence can develop through the personal growth and establishes difference between level the happiness in different countries. It is inversely proportional to the level of life.

E. VALUES OF UNEMPLOYMENT: it is contrary to the index of job; the work constitutes every person's right and is to owe of the governments to generate and protect it. The lack of job is converted in all manner of delinquency and cause of frustration and obstacle for the development well-being townspeople. If index of unemployment is bigger, the quality of life is little.

F. LIFE EXPECTANCY: people educated, employed, health and happy life can extend his existence in shape worthy. To bigger life expectancy, better quality of live.

G. PERCEPTION OF CORRUPTION: the corruption is like the AIDS to the country; the ranking is prepared by **INTERNATIONAL TRANSPARENCY** with base in specialist studies published periodically. Is cause of social non—justice and great generator of violence. The relation is contrary to the level of quality of life

H. INDEX OF PRODUCTIVITY: it represents the relation among the quantity of manufactured goods and services produced and the used resources. This index combines qualitative and quantitative aspects like value hour, applied technology, technical education, environmental conditions etc. It relation is directly proportional at the level as quality of life and the ranking is bring by international institution.

I. COUNTRY RISK: measured by international agencies considering: level of security, economic handling, panorama enterprise, conjectural political situation, labor relations, and treatment to the foreign investment, among others. It is an indicator very used by the investors and its relation is contrary to the quality level of life.

J. CONNECTIONS TO INTERNET / INHABITANT: it is an indicator very important in the world modern, because it gives idea of the grade of culture, facilities of communication, expectations of business, grade of technological development, facilities of investment, level of knowledge and information, among others. The relation is directly proportional at the same level as development of a country.

3. PROCEDURE

a. Using the ten variable chosen and concerting with minimum seven expert's in distinct areas of knowledge, make the perceptual distribution indicating the relative importance of every variable (each examiner independent distributes the 100 % of the whole, in ten variables).

b. Straightaway we appraise the variable statistically choosing best-suited for each one (arithmetical measured average, fashion or median).

c. To make the matrix with chosen countries and values belonging of every one item.

d. To distribute proportionally, the number of points out every variable according to the range of variation (maximum and minimum index).

e. To add up each country's points and those to arrange for the scale, which can be structure it worldwide.

4. UTILIZATION

Defined the classification of the countries with the object of taking decisions, as concerns the globalization of economy and arrange the quantification by variable for facility the decision in different categories according with that the reason of the analysis.

VARIABLES	PAÍSES % PONDE-RACIÓN	EEUU	SALVADOR	PANAMÁ	CTA RICA	NICARAGUA	CUBA	CANADÁ	MÉXICO	GUATEMALA	HONDURAS	ALEMANIA	ESPAÑA	FRANCIA	REINO UNIDO	ITALIA	SUECIA	PAÍSES BAJOS	GRECIA
1. calorías / habitante	9	6.08	8.73	8.96	8.49	8.32	8.90	7.27	7.27	8.28	8.49	6.89	6.07	6.27	7.15	6.51	7.22	7.31	5.90
2. mortalidad infantil	10	4.41	4.76	1.44	2.61	0.55	3.99	5.91	5.88	4.35	0.96	5.00	4.29	4.29	5.00	4.29	6.00	5.00	3.75
3. ingreso per cápita (US$)	25	17.69	1.02	1.74	1.47	0.23	0.66	12.63	1.75	0.76	0.42	16.27	8.09	14.81	11.05	11.20	14.49	14.62	6.46
4. índice de Escolaridad	6	5.94	4.56	5.46	5.70	3.96	5.76	5.82	5.34	3.90	4.20	6.00	5.94	6.00	6.00	5.94	6.00	6.00	5.94
5. tasa de empleo	8	7.97	7.38	6.96	7.58	6.40	7.56	7.90	7.81	7.40	5.76	7.22	6.40	6.98	7.43	7.00	7.36	7.55	7.22
6. Esperanza de vida	10	8.61	7.76	8.39	8.43	7.64	7.34	8.83	7.96	7.36	7.78	8.52	8.67	8.75	8.57	8.69	8.72	8.66	8.68
7. percepción de la corrupción	9	7.43	3.52	3.62	4.40	2.35	0.00	8.71	3.62	2.84	2.64	7.24	6.85	6.55	8.12	5.38	8.80	8.61	4.11
8. índice de productividad	9	9.00	4.50	4.50	4.50	4.50	4.50	8.10	3.24	4.50	4.50	1.08	2.07	2.25	1.71	2.88	0.72	0.45	2.70
9. riesgo país	8	6.73	6.23	5.78	6.16	4.15	4.90	6.66	5.45	5.57	5.02	7.35	5.96	7.20	7.09	5.84	5.99	7.22	4.04
10. conexiones a internet	6	2.05	0.05	0.19	0.40	0.06	0.03	2.50	0.17	0.04	0.04	1.77	0.83	0.87	1.83	1.39	2.77	1.48	0.57
	100	75.92	48.51	47.04	49.75	38.16	43.65	74.31	48.47	44.99	39.80	67.33	55.15	63.97	63.95	59.11	68.07	66.90	49.36

PAÍS	PUNTAJE	PAÍS	PUNTAJE
SUIZA	78.43	TAIWAN	47.04
EEUU	75.92	PANAMÁ	47.04
CANADÁ	74.31	THAILAND	46.63
NORUEGA	73.90	GUATEMALA	44.99
SINGAPORE	71.56	ARGENTINA	44.45
SUECIA	68.07	PHILIPPINES	44.00
ALEMANIA	67.33	VENEZUELA	43.88
PAÍSES BAJOS	66.90	CUBA	43.65
JAPAN	66.44	PERU	43.62
FRANCIA	63.97	CHINA	42.98
REINO UNIDO	63.95	BRASIL	41.88
ITALIA	59.11	ECUADOR	41.18
ESPAÑA	55.15	COLOMBIA	39.81
KOREA, REP.	53.86	HONDURAS	39.80
CHILE	51.05	BOLIVIA	39.01
CTA RICA	49.75	NICARAGUA	38.16
GRECIA	49.36	PARAGUAY	35.09
URUGUAY	49.36	INDIA	31.12
SALVADOR	48.51	PAKISTAN	30.60
MÉXICO	48.47	NEPAL	21.65

SUIZA	NORUEGA	COLOMBIA	BRASIL	VENEZUELA	PERU	ECUADOR	ARGENTINA	PARAGUAY	CHILE	BOLIVIA	URUGUAY	CHINA	INDIA	JAPAN	KOREA REP.	NEPAL	PAKISTAN	PHILIPPINES	SINGAPORE	TAIWAN	THAILAND
6.66	6.87	5.83	7.97	8.59	7.33	8.71	7.33	8.38	8.71	7.54	8.18	7.30	8.63	7.79	6.97	7.65	8.64	8.53	0.00	0.00	8.51
6.00	6.00	1.30	0.94	1.55	0.94	0.88	1.72	1.29	2.97	0.52	2.17	0.70	0.42	5.00	3.33	0.37	0.34	0.86	10.00	7.50	1.15
25.00	19.45	1.14	2.02	2.43	1.17	0.75	2.10	0.81	2.59	0.56	3.38	2.03	0.97	13.02	7.10	0.62	1.13	1.97	14.83	9.30	3.44
6.00	6.00	4.38	4.80	3.90	4.80	4.62	4.98	3.84	4.68	4.20	4.74	4.92	3.00	6.00	5.88	2.16	2.34	5.64	5.46	0.00	5.64
7.66	7.67	6.91	7.23	6.92	7.24	7.16	6.54	2.24	7.34	7.41	6.76	7.76	0.00	7.65	7.37	0.00	0.00	7.23	7.60	7.78	7.64
8.73	8.12	8.00	7.44	8.11	7.67	7.67	8.22	7.78	8.44	7.00	8.22	7.89	6.89	8.89	8.00	6.33	7.00	7.44	8.56	8.33	7.67
8.22	8.41	3.72	3.91	2.74	4.01	2.25	3.42	0.98	7.34	1.96	4.99	3.42	2.64	6.95	4.11	0.00	2.25	2.84	9.00	5.77	3.13
0.90	1.80	4.14	2.79	4.32	4.50	4.50	3.87	4.50	2.16	4.50	4.50	2.97	3.69	2.34	2.52	4.50	4.50	3.60	7.20	1.62	3.42
7.45	6.59	4.26	4.59	5.08	5.37	4.56	5.85	5.22	5.81	5.24	5.74	5.88	4.85	6.56	6.14	0.00	4.40	5.72	7.11	6.73	5.79
1.80	2.97	0.13	0.18	0.24	0.59	0.09	0.41	0.04	1.01	0.09	0.67	0.11	0.03	2.25	2.44	0.01	0.01	0.16	1.81	0.00	0.23
78.43	73.90	39.81	41.88	43.88	43.62	41.18	44.45	35.09	51.05	39.01	49.36	42.98	31.12	66.44	53.86	21.65	30.60	44.00	71.56	47.04	46.63

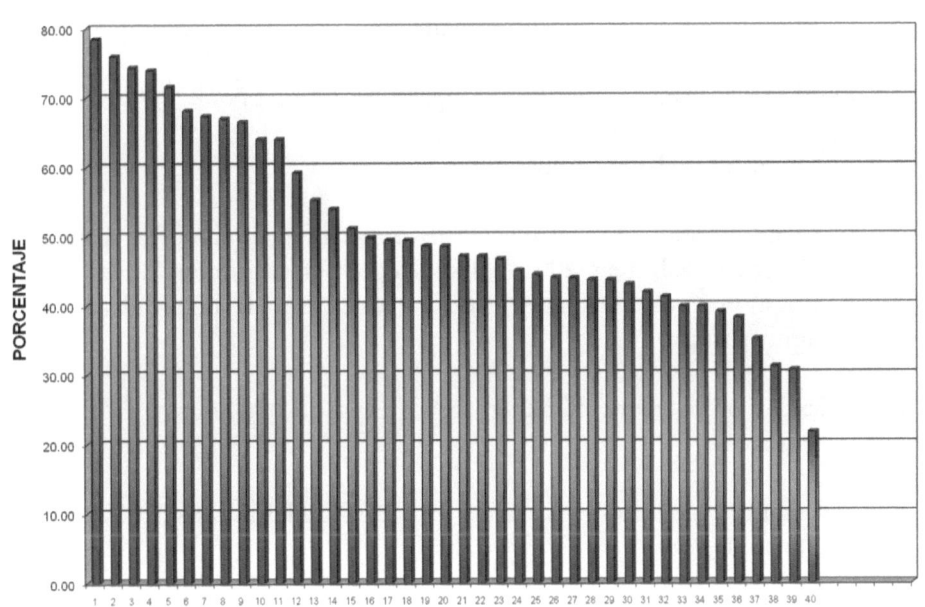

CALIDAD DE VIDA PAÍS

Information taken from:

- www.camnet.com
- www.unicef.org
- www.tvazteca.com
- www.globalcorruptionreport.org
- www.prsgroup.com
- www.sirem.com.mx
- www.worldbank.org
- www.transparencyinternacional.org
- www.onu.org

World-wide almanac 2000

1. Calories/Day/Inhabitant. Daily average of calories per capita (kilocalories) 1992-1994. World Resource Institute 1999, pp 288-9.

2. Infantile loss of life. Number of Infants by 1.000 births.

3. Per-cap it entrance. GDP per capita data source: 1999 company World Fact book.

4. Level of literacy World Health Organization, Report 1999, and p 84-87.

5. Level of use. Data source: 1999 company World Fact book.

6. Life expectancy. Total number of years.

7. Level of corruption. Annual index of perception of corruption, Transparency the International. Year 2001. Global report of corruption. Index CPI (Corruption perceptions index) has a rank between 10 (highly clean) and 0 (highly corrupt).

8. Index of productivity. Ranking ace of April 2001. Source: IMD the International.

9. Risk country. Composite risk rating June 1999. Index between 10 (without risks) and 0 (risky).

10. Connections to Internet/inhabitant. Year 2000.

Chapter 2

INTELLECTUAL CAPITAL

1. AN ATTEMPT OF MEASUREMENT

The intellectual capital presents complex problems to the relation between the management and the accounting. The specialist in administration appreciate the human resource like the more important for the entrepreneur; in the practice, the situation is very different and the treatment not always is according with this concept. The accounting is delayed in relation with the development of business and practically ignored his value, because not takes care of him, and no include it, at less in the notes to balance sheet.

Each one has personal knowledge that is intrinsic and everyone is free to utilize it for good or for bad, depending of their attitude. One entrepreneur can has the intention to buy all that he like to the worker, but no his attitude; he need gain it. If the companies cannot acquire a dominion on the human being, how can activate it? The assets are characterizes for his identity; legally belong to the company and his potential capability to generate income (cash flow).

Retake previous concepts: none asset individually considered is able to produce income. An operation requires a combination of actives (generally fixed and current) complement which administration developed by human beings. The potentially efficiency of the company depends to the capability to generate cash.

The administration will be more efficient depending of own culture, capacity intellectual of the people and the proper formation human being and, plus a specific knowledge, which requires grand investments entrepreneurial. The performance takes place to medium and long term; it is necessary to implement **a culture that canalizes all know to the company, properly protected**.

Now, the intellectual capital and his importance is accepted, especially for the virtual companies, which depend of the human being (knowledge and confidence); the alternative is attempt his measurement, development that certainly, will take long time to be accepted universally like value measure. The theme is extremely complex and has implications that will bring real and tangible benefits for the development, in general.

Dare to present one point of departure to talk about the subject, in the expectation of receiving from somebody, complementary contributions that help structure a method that resists analysis and achieve a level of acceptance that permit register his value in the balance sheet.

2. FACTORS

A. LEVEL OF PERSONAL GROWTH: investment made in the human growth with a result properly evaluated. It is measures for the amount of currency units inverted, if the results are positive, complement according to the people's academic level that integrates the organization and the investment in it.

B. EMOTIONAL COEFFICIENT THE COMPANY PERSONNEL'S: measured for experts in the theme utilizing a systematic procedure that permits taking corrective actions. It is measures for the amount of inverted currency units and people's percentage judicious people's that considers acceptable.

C. DEGREE OF SATISFACTION OF THE LABOR GROUP: it is generated for the alternatives offer for being work humanly and the possibility of realization like cultural and academics activities complemented with sports. It is measured for the investment to achieve it and the level of satisfaction using opinion polls arranged by experts.

D. COMPANY POSITIONING IN THE MIDDLE: variable to evaluate with studies of market properly certified. It is measures by the monetary unit's investment and the level of results.

E. DEGREE OF ACCEPTANCE ON THE PART OF THE COMMUNITY: calculated by means of opinion polls elaborated with a systematic procedure that he be useful for taking corrective actions. It is measure by the investment in monetary units and the results.

F. STANDARDS OF WORLDWIDE RECOGNITION:

- ISO 9000
- ISO 14000
- ISO 18000

The world has recognized and specialized institutions that bring the certified to the companies that approve the texts design for this goal and make the period maintained. The initial investment requires for obtaining it and others outcome for maintenance that must quantify in currency units.

G. RELATIONS WITH THE STATE:

- District attorneys
- Ground rules

It is measured verifying the fulfillment of commitments regulated by the status that constitute requirements to operate.

H. PRACTICES OF ASSOCIATION GOVERNMENT: it measures according to the manifest expression of the fulfillment correspondent regimentation.

I. ENVIRONMENT RULE: it measures according to the manifest expression of the fulfillment correspondent regimentation.

The company as a whole has a superior to value equity in books, defined in countable terms like the difference among active and passive totals.

Variables 1-6 measure in terms of investment executed, but given to the expenses and absolute value that fits up according to the inflation.

Variables 7, 8 and 9 have a qualitative value that for each one would be **I**

The value of the intellectual capital would be exposed in the following form, examples:

a. I—200 it fulfills a norm legal and it has invested to $200 million in intellectual capital.

b. II—300 it fulfills two norms legal and it has invested to $300 million in intellectual capital.

c. III—400 it fulfills three norms legal and it has invested to $300 million in intellectual capital.

d. III—600 it fulfills three norms legal and it has invested to $600 million in intellectual capital.

3. CALCULATION

The base is the **Q of Tobin,** calculated by the relation between the actual value of the share in the stock market and the intrinsic value. If is positive it means that the investors are paying one intangible than it does not reflect in balance. Maybe, the bookkeeping registered the previous investments like expenses:

$$Pr = A - P + I$$

Pr: real patrimony
A: asset
P: liability
I: investments in intellectual capital

$$\frac{Pr}{VM} = 2.5$$

VM: Actual value

Q of tobin **2.0**

$$VCI \text{ (josavere)} = \frac{VAICI}{\text{Company capital cost}}$$

VCI: value of the intellectual capital
VAICI: added value of the investment in intellectual capital

Chapter 3

ACCOUNTING AND COMPANIES OF CENTURY XXI

1. GENERAL CHARACTERISTICS OF THE MIDWAY

A. GLOBALIZATION: the change is a phenomenon that present permanently and with rhythm much more accelerated in the last years, especially by the advances in telecommunications and information technology, that facility the world interchange; is IRREVERSIBLE.

B. DIGITAL REVOLUTION: now it is spoken of a "net generation". We are living surrounded in a world digitalizes.

C. VERY COMPLEX MARKETS: the globalization that makes easy the information to the consumer and he turns it more opened, more demanding in his habits of purchase and of course, more rational.

D. ECOLOGICAL CONSCIENCE: the realignment run worldwide, in addition to quantitative growths looks for qualitative results that guarantees a better standard of living and the preservation of the environment.

The IMF, the BIRF and IDB condition the approval of credits to environmental policies. The standard ISO 14000, establish the minimal conditions that the companies have to consider in that matter.

E. TECHNOLOGY: becomes an application of knowledge; the advance accelerated of the last years and that is foreseen for the proximate, demands great capability of executives to understand it, to know to appreciate the opportunities that expand and to do fast changes.

F. SPEED: the mentioned characteristics demand great promptness to understand the information, to process it and to take correct decisions. The human talent will give comparative advantage, if he is capable of making good use of the basic tools for competitiveness: knowledge and information, with height grade of invention.

G. GLOBAL FINANCE: the technological development makes enormously easy the possibility to interact with any city of the world.

The investors, that are voracious, find too many possibilities of the **internet** and the **electronic bank,** systems without caring about the place where encounter the opportunities because they act through virtual companies from any place; require big capitals to finance the new technology, the research and development; achieving the positioning on the market; doing the investments that the preservation of the environment requires; developing and capacitating the human resource and attaining the sizes that the big impose multinational that have penetrated into all countries.

By means of scissions is easy the specialization that makes efficient processes; mergers to achieve economies of scale and to complement with alliances strategies to survive.

2. NEW BUSINESS—GENERAL CHARACTERISTICS

a. There are based on the **capable people** to use the technology and reinventing products and services. The employees must take part in the company's development.

b. **Specialization and great size:** family enterprise's imposes opening itself: there will be no groups directed by a head or a family; need directors specialized with information systems, communication and measurement of results to very detailed levels. There will be great pressure for efficiency.

c. **Generation of valor:** a lot of flexibility, dynamism, use of technology, invention and great capability to produce effective as a result of a permanent **generation of valor**; are required, understanding as such, the real growth of the equity and his reflection in the share value with tall index of stock-exchange.

There will be great pressure for efficiency like base to penetrate into international markets and to attract investors.

Due to the scarcity of capital in many countries, foreign investment is required. In New York's bag (year 2002) or Wall Street, worldly financial symbol, where are registered 1.600 the companies require themselves like requisite of entrance, pre-tax earnings for US $ 2, 5 million; minimum, one million stocks in circulation among the public; tangible net assets of US$ 16 million and for the less 2,000 shareholders that they have a peak of 100 stock each one.

We must go materializing those models of balance, structure of capital and status of results to be able to take part in grand financial markets in search of investors.

3. NEW EXECUTIVES— CHARACTERISTIC FEATURES

They need high level of preparation to understand it; to be of global projection; recursive, imaginative, innovative and flexible to become adapted to surprise changes and unless affects them in his emotional equilibrium for levels of pressure; must be specialist in planning practical solutions; getting ahead of events; being authentic leaders, understanding as such the help capacity; big humanists; giving enough importance to his family life, to his hobbies, and to sports and cultural activities; require great capability to motivate the work of group; domain various languages; knowing the development of business at several countries; must be familiar with the internet, tool that he permits to grow without very much infrastructure and, above all they need great capability to take decisions with a lot speed, principal characteristic of modern life.

Boards of directors need to know the business; to be able to obey a staff function and being like a true support, and no a critic of administration.

4. NEW COUNTABLE FOCUS

A. UNIVERSAL STANDARDS: it is necessary to participate active in the structuring of accounting standards of worldwide application and to give directory to go adjusting the bookkeeping in all countries, particularly in the treatment of items than long time ago, have true character of investment.

If we talked about business for a world globalization, the bookkeeping has to define some standards or universal accounting principles. According to The Wall Steel's information, in 1993 Daimler Benz before his fusion with Chrysler he announced net earnings of US$ 346 million under accounting standards of Germany. If he had used North American standards, he would have losses for 1000 million.

B. RE-FOCUS OF THE TAX DIRECTION: if **human talent** constitutes the comparative advantage for the century XXI, it will be necessary to look for mechanisms that permit calculating his value with measurements that they have worldwide acceptance like present for Edvinsson and Malone in his book: The Capital Intellectual. For human growing, the companies require grand investments; is necessary that the accounting standards make the change.

People **are they must important** in the **generation of valor**; logically, will be necessary to give the step to the **salaries of risk** with objective measurements to not incur in unbalances for predictable situations. The same problems presents with investments in preservation of the environment, the positioning, the research and development, the knowledge and the information, themes of whom right now begins to speak in some European countries. The pertinent reform in tax legislation to make the new epoch suitable is required.

C. SIMPLICITY: advancing in the search of mechanisms for implemental the salaries of risk, the vast majority of labor force including high-level executives that are extraneous to accountancy, but will be affected by the results. We needed to look for standards of measure clearly comprehensible and manageable for most people.

The result statement must compare with **foreseen** in the plan of valor generation of valor, that must become elaborate with the contest of **responsibility centers** and the constitute the key element for the evaluation of steps and a guide for investors, that need information that permit comparing the company's expectations to the alternatives that offer the national and international markets.

D. OPPORTUNITY: nowadays, computers are tools of common use. Great quantities of shareholders know the results of exercise very later that impedes performing with the speed that circumstances impose.

The administration must take control of the situation and congregating all of the stakeholders and affected to discuss new-filed dates of been financiers in agreement with the midways that we have to our reach.

Assemblies must be deliberative forums that present results compared with projections to go constructing indicators of credibility that be used as guide for the investment and to define the distribution of dividends based in the projection of cash flow.

Chapter 4

APPLICATION OF THE STATISTICS TO THE FINANCES

Statistic is the science that deals with the harvesting, arrangement, analysis, interpretation and presentation, of data corresponding to an experiment previously planned or defined, or an accumulated historical situation in a series of data to handle.

In the application to subjects of financial nature, like in all the other fields, we must take care of the results by use of unsuitable data, false hypotheses, erroneous relations, partiality mathematical errors. In other words, we must use in suitable form so valuable tool for the decision making. It is required to become aware of the mathematical preparation necessary to be able to incursion in the use of advanced models of prediction.

The most common applications in finance are:

1. FINANCIAL ANALYSIS

a. **Rotation of inventories:** expressed in days.

b. **Inventory average** = (initial inventory + final inventory)/2

This type of analysis is very deceptive, especially when the business has stationary sales which force to accumulate existence to take care of the seasons.

In addition the final inventory to the period base becomes the initial inventory of the following and so on, which takes use of erroneous data (programmed for yearend).

The use of monthly numbers of inventory and to divide by twelve to obtain an average, appears unless **a mode,** or that most recommendable is a **medium** one, which does not consider the extreme values.

a. **Rotation of accounts to receive and accounts to pay:** for these cases, the analysis is identical to previous and very especially for companies with stationary sales and special concessions for the final of the year, very common situation.

Particularly, in case of accounts to receive he is much more correct to apply an indicator more dynamic than it consists of dividing the total value of the portfolio by the average daily of sales on credit and multiplied by the days of term that grants the company. Example:

Balance of accounts to receive: $900.000.000

Term of sales: 90 days

term of sales: 90 days

$$\frac{\text{sales of last the 90 days}}{90 \text{ days}} = \frac{1.000'000.000}{90}$$

Balance of accounts to receive = 112 million

$$\text{days of portfolio} = \frac{\text{accounts to receive}}{112'000.000} = \frac{900'000.000}{112'000.000} = 8 \text{ days}$$

b. **Term average of accounts to pay:** it is come from way very similar; knowledge directly with an example:

Term average suppliers = 52 days

Last purchases 52 days = 104 million

$$\text{purchases average day} = \frac{104'000.000}{52 \text{ days}} = 2'000.000$$

Balance of accounts to pay = 130 million

$$\text{days of accounts to pay} = \frac{130'000.000}{2'000.000} = 65 \text{ days}$$

Note that the days of accounts to receive and to pay calculated of the previous way represent the updated behavior more and dynamic than can be obtained using the statistic correctly.

2. FORECASTS

The investor to run greater risk if the profit expectation is greater; the investments of variable rent, as its name indicates, do not have certainty of a yield and therefore is due to consider, running the risk of calculate by the difficulties practical to predict future income.

Very commonly economic scenes with categories are defined:

- situation of crisis
- growth medium
- stop growing

To which one assigns occurrence probabilities to them. It is a bad procedure because the process is not random. When threw a currency to the air we have the certainty that falls by face or seal and therefore can assign probabilities of occurrence. The economic phenomena obey to a series of variables whose study is of governmental character and specialized organizations using the correct indicators for each case.

To the executives corresponds analyze the type of predictions carefully, to see if they deserve credibility and to complement with his himself judgment. Comparing different sources of intelligence and verifying results is possible to be constructing **indicating of credibility** that give to objective criteria for their future use.

3. MATRIX OF SECTOR GROWTH

Each company must construct a matrix of the sector growth, considering the sectors with those interact and the perspective that glimpse the specialists in the theme to foretell the macroeconomic expectations.

Once the company elaborates the **"matrix of josavere"** or the sector growth, must enter to look for the **applicable economic indicators** for its particular situation using the analysis of multiple correlation.

So far let us of the construction of the matrix of the sector growth. Steps to follow:

1. To carefully select the sectors with those who we interacted in the economy.
2. With base in the calculated projections, transcribe the indicators.
3. To establish the percentage participation of the sales in each sector (based in recent statistics).
4. Using Excel, calculated the average.

Example: the MMM S.A. interacts with the sectors that acquire knowledge in the matrix.

Sector	Participation % in the Sectors Po Year	Sector Perspective of Growth P1 Year	Weighed growth P1 Year
* Warehouses of chain	10	8	80
* Fast meals and restaurants	15	12	180
* Confectioneries and chocolate factory	18	5	90
* Cakes, snack and cereals	12	7	84
* Milky	10	4	40
* Bakery and Confectioner's shop	25	12	300
* Transport of passengers	10	3	30
	100	TOTAL GROWTH	0.04

The growth prospected in real terms 8, 04% multiplied by the inflation perspective, gives the minimum growth average expected in the company by effects of the economic growth. For the example: 8.04% * .1, 09 = 8, 76%, assuming a projected inflation of 9% for the period to elaborate.

4. PROJECTION OF SALES

This is the **key** decision, without a doubt, to formulate plans of generation of value. If by error, the projection is underestimated, forecast losses and vice verse.

A. MODELS ECONOMETRICS: it is one system or more equations than describe to the relation between economic variables and series of time. It is the case of the simple linear regression that it represents the growth of the sales with the time passage.

$$y = b + (m * x)$$

y: sales
b: interception of x in y
m: slope
x: years (1,2,3, ... n)

The multiple correlations consider the number of variables that affect the result of the sales:

$$y = a_1 x_1 + a_2 x_2 + a_3 x_3 + \ldots a_n x_n$$

Models nonlinear which are but complex and applicable in special cases

B. QUALITATIVE MODELS: it is used in the case of new products or when it is not had information. It consists of the use of subjective appreciation; it can be:

a. **Panel of experts** with well directed independent criterion and. He must take control of personnel of the company and the aid of external advisers.

b. **Historical analogies** using situations that are presented in the company in previous periods.

c. **Investigation of markets** identifying the prospective buyers.

The executives choose the model that more adjusts to the particular situation; it must complement with **the criterion of the work team**. The models simply provide the point to begin; to understand the statistic of another way, constitutes one serious error.

5. ANALYSIS OF RISK

In finance investment defined the risk like the possibility of change in relation to an awaited value; it can be negative or positive. Usually is assumed that the possible yields are according distribution normal which has the following characteristics:

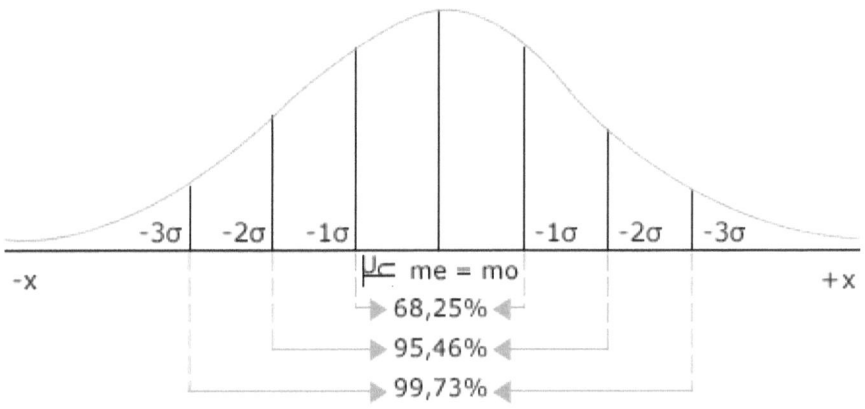

It has bell form:

- Is symmetrical in relation to the average
- It is continuo
- The average, medium and the mode are equal.
- It is always positive (no short x-axis)
- more or less has two points of flexion in s
- It is applied to populations whose value tends to infinite

The normal distribution is characterized by the knowledge of the average and the standard deviation and obeys the following law of concentration of data:

a. In interval X ± 1ç is the 68, 26% of all the values samples.

b. In interval X ± 2ç are 95, 46% of all the values samples.

c. In interval X ± 3ç are 99, 73% of all the values samples.

In statistic the dispersion (degree of amplitude of the company) with the standard deviation is moderate which mathematically is expressed like:

$$\sigma = \sqrt{\sum_{i-1}^{\Sigma} (x_i - x)^2 \, px}$$

    s: standard deviation
    x_i: variable
    x: average
    px: probability of occurrence

ç is taken like one first approach of the measurement of the risk.

Coefficient of variation is equivalent to the division of the standard deviation by the average or awaited value.

$$CV = \varsigma \, / \, m$$

    CV: coefficient of variation
    ç: standard deviation
    m: average sample

The best approach is considered to measure the risk. If two mutually excluding projects, have the same average or expected value with different standard deviation, the more risked is the greater deviation.

The important is to determine if the distribution is applicable to the particular phenomenon which we are analyzing (cash flow, dividends to receive, value of the share in the stock-market, etc.) and that with the previous values can be reasonably calculated the probability of occurrence of a phenomenon, in the measurement that behavior follows a distribution normal; an example:

If the awaited yield "mediates" is of 16% and the standard deviation of 9%, it indicates that with a 68% of probability, the yield will be between 7 and 25% (16 ± 9).

The measurement of the risk, using the normal distribution, is related to the inherent risk the investments; the concept has much of intuitive, the investor moves in an ample rank defined by:

a. Minimum risk: in theory, one Treasury bond of the government of the U.S.A. (low yield but completely fixes). Now this concept is discountable

b. Bonds sweepings: (junk bonds) which are emitted by companies in reconstruction process (leaving a crisis). The payment of interests this subject to a positive result, reason why is an interest rate superior to the one of the market but with greater risk.

When the markets are **sufficiently ample** becomes the analysis beta (ß) introduced by Sharpe, which consists of finding the standard deviation of the results waited for in the market like a whole so that it serves as pattern of comparison with the beta of an share in particular. If the beta of the share is greater than the one of the market, the share is very volatile (risky) and vice versa.

$$ßshare > ßmarket$$

It indicates that the share varies more than proportionally to the total variation of the market and if the relation is smaller (< 1) indicates the opposite.

Previously explained he is applicable to the unique risk of the company which commonly is called **non-systematic** risk, which is **diversifiable**. The risk of the market is not **diversifiable; it cannot be eliminated** in the same country.

Risk country calculates based on the security, the economic handling, the enterprise panorama, the relevant to now, political situation, the labor relations, the treatment to the investment and other factors.

6. INVESTMENT DECISIONS

In finances a generalized and respected principle exists: **not to place all eggs in the same basket,** which in the current language is equivalent to say that one must diversify the investments.

For practical effects, the correlation coefficient constitutes the measurement tool and it calculates as it indicates in *Projections I* and *Projections II*. It is interpreted thus:

1. < r is a value between—1 r <1

2. **One value next to—1,** indicates discharge negative correlation; the positive results of one(s) variable one(s) imply negative results in the other(s)

3. **One value next to +1** implies discharge positive correlation; the positive results of one(s) variable one(s) also imply positive results in the other or the other variables.

In the case of portfolio of investments one is to look for an optimal combination between yield and risk.

Chapter 5

HAPPINESS AND PRODUCTIVITY

1. THE VALUABLE GENERATION AND THE GRADE OF HAPPINESS

There are a direct relation among the grade of happiness of human teams of company and the level of productivity. Using one study prepared for "The Great pleases to Work" the companies that occupy the first places in the grade scale has the characteristic present in summarize, for check in a real situation

The workers perceive like the more important aspects, the ones that help to make the workplace pleasantly the following:

- The vision and honesty his leader's.
- The information that they receive of his directors.
- The attitude toward equilibrium among labor and personnel life.
- Pride for the company and his corporate image.
- The grade of autonomy that are offered.
- The attitude with respect to the delegation to take decisions.
- The possibility that it be offered to them to appeal in unbalanced situations.
- Recognition to work and to the individual effort.
- The environment of comradeship in the working party.
- A just compensation than good administrated, helps him to improve his standard of living.

The summary, of general policies of the better companies to work according to the document, in the same order are:

1. A&: the best place to work in one country; drives a scheme turned on participation, without favoritisms; ample communication; great importance to open capacitate and foments the bilingualism; utilize the incentives for performance and results. Equity in internal promotions and people without tied-up; opportunity to do profession with international interchanges and opportunities to family leisure. Entrusts in the work to accomplish without agreed extras (the rest is surcharge or inefficiency).

2. B&: multinational that respect the individual; toasts opportunity of professional development; excellent communication; ethical behavior; incentive the performance; permanent capacitating (e-learning) and flexible working day; Worry for well-being the worker's and his families.

3. C&: Height compensation trough salaries, incentives and benefits; respect the workpeople with tall level of requirement in productivity; toasts opportunity of professional plan including capacitating; worry about upgrading the worker's life and his family utilizing employees' funds and the mutual fund of investment. The communications are fluid; people with very good relations and equilibrium in labor and family life; reward economically the directors that proven expectations.

4. D&: multinational enterprise that offers good environment of work; opportunities of development; sincere communication; plans of recognition with benefits for employees and opportunity to have influence to the exterior. Bring opportunity of flextime and impartiality in processes; bring especial activities including the families; programs of recognition with incentives and bonuses with special price for results.

5. E&: management of the performance; arranges for a development plan for each worker; Equilibrium among personal and labor life, including the families: people work for living, do not live to work. The employs **must not** remain working after the time of departure; programs of recognition and incentives with possibility to do race out-of-doors.

6. F&: multinational enterprise that take care of the equilibrium among personal and labor life of the workers; worried because his employees perform a good work with high remuneration, leisure, recognition, capacitating and development; impartiality in processes; policies of remuneration largely diffuse with incentive plans of motivations, incentive and rewards.

7. H&: multinational that maintains a plan of succession that guarantees development and clearings for performance and possibilities of internationalization all of the workpeople's; worry about the person and his family and the equilibrium among labor and family life; open-door policy and impartiality in processes.

8. I&: promotes the technical and human development of employees to generate the motivation orientated to achieve the goals. For them, working is the pleasure to be a member of a company that trusts imagination and the contribution of wholes; the technical development, human promote and social of his employees. Programs of recognition and rewards to surpass the goals; they take care of the equilibrium among personal and labor life; they practice the management of the performance of his workers.

9. J&: base the strategy in open interest, management autonomy and recognitions with incentives to run. They offer confidence and they appreciate his collaborators whom capacitate to work as a team; procure Integrate the family and the equilibrium among labor life and personnel life; offer flexibility in work periods and obvious procedures.

10. K&: bases the strategy management in meritocracy and recognitions because people is the key resource; integrate the family; do evaluation of performance with measurements with participation the less seven persons; reward the accomplishments, the best team of work and the best boss of area.

11. L&: bases his steps on activities, goals and objectives that individual commitments periodically evaluated, divulged and turned into properly motivated. The people are the key resource. The human steps are borne in recognition, the technical capacitating and program them of well-being of the employee and his family group.

12. M&: multinational with all kinds of freedoms if the drawn objectives which it is tracking and clearings on come true. Each employee updates his annually development plan with human resources. Impartiality in processes; bring a lot of freedom to develop his workpeople's potential and offer promotional opportunities to the exterior.

13. **N&:** multinational that offers respect for the individual and opportunity to grow labor. The worker's physical and emotional equilibrium are promoted, including the family. They drive plans of recognition and incentives for performance and procedures of public knowledge to avoid favoritisms.

14. **O&:** offers job security; impartiality in processes, good environment of work and excellent personal relations; impartiality in processes and programs of recognition; they think in workpeople and the family. Drive like strategy the continuous formation for own talent improving his personnel's profile and the commitment with the society; they keep jealously his works.

15. **P&:** bases the strategy in ethics, the honesty and the respect; great investment in capacitating; good labor environment; the busy personnel's culture; the opportunities of growth; freedom to say about what is thought; respect for family's time. His policy's pillars of human resources are: **a,** excellent leaders; **b,** engaged people and **c,** efficient organization; do judicious evaluation of the performance and improve; recognize the work and effort additional; offer promotional possibilities to the exterior.

16. **S&:** multinational with good environment of work; flexibility of schedules; potential of development within the organization; open doors and activities of recognition and motivation with bonuses for performance; the work as a team and passion for what they do respecting the family's time; strict handling of meritocracy.

17. **R&:** multinational with presence at one hundred forty seven countries, he bases his business in the human capital; they do all the promotions with base in meritocracy; the goal in the management development is to get to be member; flexible agreements in the workday with that tools permit being connected with the office; integrate the family and do tall recognition to the performance. Good school.

18. **T &:** great labor environment with capable leaders to understand the personal necessities of employees; sincere communication, clear and transparent; work a team with positive people; rule perfectly defined for staff, promotions, transfers, salaries and benefits; recognition with simple programs and incentives; equilibrium of personal and labor life; internal culture guided to the execution with excellence.

19. **V&:** definite clearly an ethical line and code of conduct; people with a lot of human quality that he generates confidence; offer possibility of personal

development; motivates the good performance with first extras; bring labor flexibility to balance the labor and familiar life.

Organizational challenging, demanding and competitive culture with recognitions and incentives to better performances; impartiality in processes; application of meritocracy and recognized like school of executives.

20. Z&: maintains evaluation of performance guided to detect competitions to develop including the personal; labor flexibility; impartiality in processes; incentives to recognize achievements and advances;; open-door policy; freedom to be successful; impartiality in processes; capacitating and possibilities to internationalize.

Like businessmen our worker of an organization, is important a personal reflection, based in the famous sentence of John F. Kennedy, thinking that **we can contribute for the better environment in the job** and to take it like a daily discipline, complementing with a positive attitude with respect to companions, love the work, having mentally influence to the service borrowed, concentrates in what do, **here and the now**, discipline that learns with practice and, implies **being conscious** and developing **the inner peace**.

Especial attention must take place to foment proceedings that permit achieving and maintaining the **confidence** of everybody with whom interacted, reminding that **is very fragile**.

The grade of happiness, is more an attitude contagious of the team than a selfish individual, right along conditioned the quality of relations with the other ones and of the carriage to enjoy life.

As each person must contribute his quota of happiness to the team; it is looks for oneself from within (the inside) to out, and that the factors that affect the happiness are: health, personal moral values, work, family's relations, the economic situation, the friends and the individual freedom.

Companies in turn, they must propitiate the conditions to make easy a behavior to the people that he induce **collective happiness**, to the one that all contribute to, like part of his corporate strategies and involving them in his mission, his vision and in moral values to take care of with zeal, in order that they become elements of organizational, orientated culture to generate value in the company and countries space where it operate, respecting his laws, the environment and way of life.

The index of correlation among happiness and the creative capability makes easy the appearing of the brilliant sparks required to create a **culture of invention**. This is the most easy form to exercise leadership in the sector, in order to increase the possibilities of **generation** of **valuable**, creating one environments to play and to laugh because good humor in addition to be emotional intelligence stimulates the creativity.

Meritocracy, equilibrium among labor and personnel life; the opportunities of development; the incentives to run; excellent communications and good environmental implicating the family, certainty increased conditions and constitute basic factors, very commendable to propitiate the generation of value. Bring respect and inspiring love, like the basis of emotional, spiritual and social intelligence.

2. INNOVATION

Represents the easier and practical way to surpass the competition or to become converted in leader of the sector and to improve the margins of profit, key element to increment the competitiveness.

It depends on a mental attitude at the company; a way of life and fruit of the **work of a team** directed by an **adapted leader**. Thomas D. Kuczmarski in his book "Innovation—it defines strategies for markets of tall competition", define the leader a creative person, good motivator, of easy communication, with initiative, perspicacity and experience to integrate human team, resolving conflicts; with to get involved works up with the team, giving continuous reorientation and positive print.

Of an editorial published in Portafolio in April 11/07 I extract the following concept:

"In a job of 1998, published in the magazine Organization Science, Frank J.t Barret, professor of the Naval Postgraduate School of Monterey, California, and pianist professional of jazz, underline that the bureaucratic model is not the adequate in a global economy. In order to be innovators, the managers, just like musicians, have to know how to interpret footloose indicia, to confront tasks disorganized, processing incomplete knowledge and, still in uncertain conditions, taking measures and starting the action..."

In very general terms, the creative ideas start off and develop the following steps:

- Concept or idea
- Try quantitative
- Financial projections
- Creating a prototype (research and development)
- You try of manufacture and marketing
- Presentation to sales

The success is measured in terms of products or hits of invention, which must measure oneself as indicate later on.

It is fundamental to develop a sense of curiosity, to offer additional wages and salaries, to maintain a support related to management conscientiously that many ideas do not bear fruit; maintaining the focused equipment and supplying the economic resources.

The general manager must know show that cannot be delegated; having active linkage balancing stock with words and coherent support transmitting passion, fervor and faith. Communicating with positive and decided attitude; type we can do it, in addition to his conviction that one tries of one long-term investment and the fact that his achievement does not exist a general road, rather must work at the environment own of the company in individual.

To think different is essential; but there of how they do the things today, the goods that manufacture or the services that offered. The invention can be made in: markets, new products, selling methods, forms of delivery, service pre and post-sale, systems of manufacture, forms of leadership, strategic direction, methods of compensation, and other ones.

A. ENTERPRISE CHARACTERISTICS: in addition to a manager with intention can do it that inculcate, stand out and back up an innovative intention, engaged active participant, a team with desire and passion for the invention requires, which departs of an instinct. The team's members owe:

- Having diversity of experiences.
- Being optimistic.

- Having self-confidence and creativity.
- Propensity toward the solution of problems.
- Being desirable of the people.
- Demanding and transmitting an internal passion to create new things.
- Feeling realized with the invention and the launching of new products.
- Having experienced failures and capable being to surpass them.

According to Thomas D. KUCZMARSKI, these the groups that integrate with a careful procedure of selection for periods of one or two years, must meet regularly in with previous programming of several classrooms. Once a week in meetings of four hours in addition to others including breakfasts, lunches and foods of work; Encounters of one or two days at different places to the one belonging to chores to strengthen the relation and to stimulate the creativity. The members of the team in addition to good clearings and recognitions must have obvious his future once finish off his participation.

B. MEASUREMENT: basic complement to generate the **innovative culture** is the objective measurement of results for signs that they may work out, especially in the first stages of his development. A model is required to utilize and to check in shape systematic to learn from experience.

would to start entering in books the investment; accomplishing which limit must do; use of financial resources having in account of experimentation; demand capital; the participation of new products in total sales and the margin of contribution to calculate a profitability index. Besides doing periodic evaluation of the performance of the members of the group and doing feedback.

C. IMPLEMENTATION: it is recommended initiating with a summit meeting, with all the solemnity of the case to train some apostles from carefully selected candidates; thus beginning the process and circumscribing actions that keep alive wit; is needed and is convenient to increment the grade of happiness to stimulate the interaction of nerve cells and to improve the creative capability.

Chapter 6

APPROACHES TO PERSONAL QUALITY

INTRODUCTION

A characteristic clearly defined in the modern world is change. We could say that the human being does not adapt, lives against the flow and psychologically it is exposed to a death earlier than the physical one.

The entrepreneurs, who loves subsist, don't have another way that the constant search of mechanisms to improve the quality within the norms established, accepting the premise: **"the quality is designed and made"**.

Starting off from the very possible human errors, the enterprises must orient themselves to find perfection by means of systems that allow the interaction of the workers and the used mechanisms in order **to prevent,** any possible, displace in relation to the established norms and to facilitate remedial actions.

If we accepted that "nobody can give what he does not have", it becomes impossible to speak of total quality, if the people who works in a company does not have it.

The first preoccupation has to be which the development of the human resource, as it contributes to improve the quality of life, forming useful people for the society and, productive to the company in particular. Thus little by little, we will be creating an enterprise culture based on quality criterion, having as a priority the people.

In this order of ideas, display initially the principles of life, frame of reference to obtain the happiness of the workers, base so good labor, through which the great humanists call **to flow**, against the term commonly used in our culture **to fight**

The work is basic for happiness; that would mean a world of people completely idle?; would not be six billion, perhaps the double or the triple; it is an excellent mechanism of personal accomplishment and one pretty opportunity to serve, **"who does not live to serve, does not deserve to live"**.

An important decision of the human consists to taste working, enjoying which he does; maintain total conscience of the opportunity that has to serve others in a direct or indirect form. Whoever, who work thus, **flow** and is happy.[1]

It corresponds to the entrepreneurs to provide the suitable atmosphere, so that the workers can be made like people; given the best to them if in his work, so that the efficiency and the quality will be **optimal.** How to obtain it?

2. PRINCIPLES OF LIVE

Many people have two mistakes of formation assignments of good faith; one of them consists of thinking that we came to this world to suffer; the natural state of a sound mind is **happiness.**

The important is to look the happy inside **ourselves**; not in the external world; we must focus in to **be human; to have,** has been the fruit of the consumer society that the enslaved people obtains things at whatever cost.

In search of that happiness, is important to analyze the life principles, with the object of improving of it. Review a schematic presentation of each one.

1. THE HEALTH: base on a pleasant life; the patients suffer and make suffer to others. In addition, the high costs of the necessary services, and the bitterness of the relatives and friends.

The concept includes the spiritual, material and the social aspects that interact looking for a balance. In order to maintain the body affluent[3] we need a

healthy mind. The brain is a computer of immense capacity; according to the experts, the person who learns to use, at least 10% of her potential, turns into a genius.

The brain has two hemispheres. The left one can do that means remember; it is like a kind of recorder that repeats when is ordered; it is the part of the memory, the most developed in the common people, fruit of the education received that ago long emphasizes in the repetition.

The right hemisphere has to do with the imaginative aspect; creativity, the initiative, the development of the mysterious. By ignorance, this part has been very little worked by humanity, wasting an excellent mechanism of growth and improvement to obtain the well-being.

By means of the use of the right hemisphere of the brain, the human beings can reach objectives such as:

- To remember and to interpret the dreams.
- To program the dream periods.
- To control the vices (alcoholism, drug addiction, etc.)
- To transform us into positive beings.
- To control weight.
- To learn to have a healthy body.
- To create abundance.
- To invent in all the fields of science and technology.
- To develop intuition.
- To develop the telepathic.
- In general, everything that has to do with esoteric sciences.

In order to learn to develop the right part, mechanism the **meditation is the best,** entering **into one** to look for the kingdom of GOD exactly where it is.

The capitalist society through the publicity has awakened on us the interest by many useless things developing in us the culture of having: "Whatever you have, whatever you're worth."

The funeral and burials bring good elements for understand a simple philosophy: who dies let all in the land; the only thing that he takes, his spiritual development that serves to respond before the Divine Justice, the only one that exists, because the human is loaded with misunderstandings, fiddles, threats, falsifications, etc.

Everything that people makes for perfect himself, as a human being cultivating goodness, tolerance, understanding, empathy, respect, patience, etc.; help to find the **inner peace**, the authentic health.

One person can deceive the others, but never will be able to **deceive himself**. Everything that goes against the inner peace goes against the health, the first principle of life.

2. THE LOVE: it is the essence, the reason of being of the whole humanity. Whoever loves, lives in a superior dimension because begins to receive love from the others. The love must be extended to the nature, taking care and preserving the environment, the species animals, vegetables and minerals. The nature doesn't ask anything and gives all; at least, we must avoid its destruction, with harmful practices to the light of the natural law.

The animals respond with affection when note that somebody loves them, including the tamer with the wild. The plants respond with flowers and fruits the affection that receives. They are subjects sufficiently treated by the specialists and it is important for the current people, the experimentation with the purpose of verifying it directly; it is very easy to observer. Take a shower in a fall; embrace to the tree in order to notices it.

The rewarding energy received embracing a tree, walking barefoot on the grass, breathing the pure air or receiving in their body directly the water that falls. Fortify yourself receiving and penetrating the solar light (without exaggerating).

Enjoy watching the moon and live the pleasant inspiration that feels observing the stars carefully; go to the beach, to understand the immensity of the world and to have a forceful test of the existence of God.

It is important take advantage of all the benefits that minerals provide through practices like bathing in the beach; to drink of thermal waters(moderate); make mud masks in all the body; experiment the rest that feels sleeping in a seated gravel or in a stone. The experts in the matter analyze with amplitude the great benefits obtains that precious stones like crystals and quartzes.

In order to satisfy the curiosity that some reader can experience, there are an ample bibliography on medicinal plants and their healing power, the benefits of the fruits; the beneficial minerals and their effects for humanity; the influence of the stars on the living human beings, etc.

The previous reflections serve to learn **love the nature**. Preserved and lived in harmony as luckily begins to understand the humanity and as note in the government programs. It is important, of course, the love by oneself and the other human beings. There are few with worth and we have to learn to love them.

One person that loves does not judge, is tolerates; accepts the others as they are; is patient with the weaknesses of the others; when has good thing shares which another; offers his services in a spontaneous manner; does not refuse when he knows that some person need it, teaches with affection; tries to include the point of view of his opponent; prayed by the others; works thinking about the benefit for others; shares the pains of the others without being called, etc.

In summary, remembering the words that Reinaldo Arroyave L., the grand teacher, "I would like reduce the ten mandates to two: the first to love God over all things and the second, to love the human as myself". This implies the care of not harming anybody and to take the advantage of any opportunity to lend a hand; we must try to turn us into a channel so that the **love of God** flows through us towards the other human beings.

3. TO GIVE: all human beings have some particular abilities in which he is superior to the others; which indicates that all the people have something to contribute to the others. Knowing oneself is the bases of wisdom; it allows us to discover our strengths and weaknesses.

Each one must contribute which the best aspect of him in benefit of the others. If each one gives the maximum that he can contribute, created abundance for all. It is question to abandon the selfishness and to think well with altruistic cause.

The most general mistake consists of giving expecting to receive something in return. That way of acting generates great frustrations because the ingratitude is very common defect the human nature.

It is important make of giving a daily custom, taking advantage of all opportunities that appear to us, beginning by something as simple how an affectionate greeting, a spontaneous attention, a sincere smile; a brotherly hug, an affectionate kiss and continuing with the material. Without telling anybody and without looking receives anything, but inspired by the Bible: "That your left hand not account what make the right hand".

In a third order, act the people who have obtained a certain degree of development that allows to pardon, to give advice, to teach, to love, to govern and in general everything what implies **leadership**, understanding it as, **the capacity to help**.

The parents remember with immense satisfaction the great joy that feels when give everything to the boy without waiting for absolutely nothing for him; they are pretty years of the childhood when the relationship father—son is very perfect,. The spontaneity of the boy to give love, to provide affection and joy are practically indescribable. It is the great happiness that feels that each one is giving the best of himself, relationship that is much more perfect between the mother and the son.

Remember prayer of Francis of Asis: given, I receive. This can be verified, simply by teaching (learning very much)

4. UNIFICATION: the universe entire is energy that appears under different forms and that never can be destroying.

The human being is a circuit of energy whose potential depends on each person individually and whose capacity we can increase based on techniques that we can learn. That energy affects and alters everything that enters in contact with the person, like the environment, the objects, the animals and others. Neither knowing how, but we are intercommunicated with all the beings in nature.

Starting off the cosmic energy, origin of the universe (God) brought forth all the human beings. The conscience is developed when a body by the fertilization, forms from the same maternal womb, stars to develop the mind, feeding it through the senses (sight, ear, sense of smell, taste and touch).

The senses of the human beings are limited, in comparison to the animals, and for that reason they are bad sensors, and offer very limited information. Thus, the mind creates judgments of values constituting the moral that is many changers depending on the particular convenience. For that reason it explains, for example, that although to kill is a heinous crime, society awards the great generals by their feats in the war.

The judgments of values constitute preconceptions of which it brings forth the thought, which constitutes a conscious manifestation.

The thought regulates the feelings. These can be pleasant, disagreeable or neutral and according to them we act. The way we act constitutes the **life**.

In summary, the human person living according to the circumstances surround him. For that reason it is very important in the development of the human being during the first years of life including, of course the days in the womb of its mother, because they mark the surroundings so that the senses inform their mind.

In studies of regression demonstrated as the immense majority of criminals are fruit of acts of pleasure, without the essential quota of love so that life blooms in entire splendor. For that reason, a balanced society, need **responsible fathers**, so that the children receive good feeding, love, education and in general, all the physical and spiritual elements for a balanced development.

The companies must create pleasant atmospheres in the work place and select positive people and try to increase their positivist by means of the different practices from their reach so that positive interrelation is radiated and contributed to flowing to what we talked before. If we change the think, we change the way we feel and everything becomes positive.

5. PARDON: the limitations of the senses are many; some occasions to feed the mind mistaken that create judge of value mistaken and we are full of prejudge, hatred, wrath, rages and other negative reactions.

If he is black, protestant, soccer player, politician, artist, etc.," he is bad". Those blazes close the mind for the entire stranger, the new thing, and the different thing and consequently it limits much a sound mental attitude.

The problem is more serious when we dragged personal resentments: I am fat, poor, long nosed, one eyed, crippled, etc., etc., that can cause limitations to develop the love for one, bases to love others and to get close to God. TO LOVE, IT IS INDISPENSABLE TO PARDON and to pardon, it is necessary to forget.

The pardon opens the doors to love and implies forgetfulness. We must start by forget ting the negative feelings that we bring from the maternal womb, continue with those of childhood and following with the most recent.

If we don't change the situation by our own mean; the best is to seek a professional psychoanalyst so that through a process of regression get rid of that; ballast that can cause much damage to us.

Pardoning ourselves, we located in the channel of the own love, bases for the self-esteem, recommend to live happy and to project to the others. As we are surpassing that stage of personal resentments, we learn to understand the problems of others and it becomes easier to pardon.

The common of people by lack of CONSCIENCE, the key to live happy, acts like my great friend Alberto Angel Botero, taught me once: "with an automatic pilot". We happened over things without giving a thought; we lived loaded on resentments and without think, we say father: pardoned our offenses as we pardoned that offended us".

And we are happy speaking about the offense received and commented which all the exaggeration looking obtaining the favor of the thirds. The assumption that we are able "to get into the other" and to decipher that he was thinking and what was the intentions etc., etc.

As after all we must interact with different people, many of them with little personal qualities, we are exposed to receive personal offended by others, in some cases and listened to those who like that we take sides in their favor (supposedly victim).

On time, and without know, we are filled of hatreds and resentments like bag ballast. That serious mistake; fill the mind of negative thoughts; remember aspect explained in UNIFICATION, principle that implies the interaction of minds.

We ourselves free of resentments can closer of God, the superior being who pardons us all and sent his son, JESUS CHRIST to pardon all our sins.

We have a miraculous formula to learn to pardon: to program the brain that only remembers the good things and to cultivate that discipline repeating consciously the words of Francis of Assis:

> "Lord, make me an instrument of your peace
> That where there is hatred, let me love,
> Where there is injury, pardon,
> Where there is doubt, faith
> Where there is despair, hope
> Where there is darkness, light
> Where there is sadness, joy.
> Oh! Divine Master!

Grant than I may not seek
To be consoled, as to console
That I may not to be understood, as to understand
That I may not seek to be loved, as to love
For it is in giving that we receive
It is in that we are pardoned
And it is in dying.
That we are born to the eternal life".

6. TO MAKE DECISIONS: making decision is inherent to life. You decide if you are a criminal or a good person, if you are a good or a bad son, if you studies or not, if are worker or a vagrant.

These are examples of the type of decisions that habitually we must make. The important is that all decision is oriented to the search of **inner peace**. Acting with that directive, hardly makes bad decisions because he never does contrary to the nature or its resemblances, whatever is the field in which he is acting.

The reading of this subject indicates that you want to improve your quality of life. That is a very important decision and implies a great amount of changes in his habits, customs and ways of behavior that initially demand much sacrifice. Surely you are not going to change overnight; a phenomenon of this type implies to be improving every day, but at the end you will be happy.

Now reflect in the seventh principle; is very mentioned by all the therapists of these subjects; according to Antony De Melo, we can learned about it through the CONSCIENCE.

G. TO LIVE THE MOMENT: to leave a pardoning ourselves and all those that offended us. Everything what happened is history and the best way to do it, is living every moment intensely whatever the activity that we make.

The human being is not able to do two things at a time; we must dedicate to do one with all our vital capacity. It is common to be in a soccer game, thinking why we not went to see another, or comparing with that which we saw some time back. To eat, thinking the misfortune; in my friend; the good meat to had the day before today. This way of acting constitutes an obstacle to be happy; when one goes to bed must forget everything and put blank the mind and the dream comes as resultant.

A person working must dedicate completely to he is doing; maintaining present the useful of the product or the service, independently of the type of the work; concentrating with all his senses and produce the maximum.

Another very common mistake, to live thinking about what will happen in the future; and worse, almost always with negative approach; the preoccupations made damage. Who life the moment don't made this mistake and surely learns to face situations calmly when they appear.

In the measurement that we life practicing these principles, like norms the happiness is coming.

---

1. For the rest of the time we will take care of it further.
2. I knew in a conference of Doctor Rosa Argentina Rivas in a national convention the Silva method under the direction of Doctor Laura Pinto. What wise people! Here I analyzed them under my personal approach.
3. On this subject an ample bibliography of medical type exists.

CHAPTER 7

INTERNATIONALIZATION AND GLOBALIZATION

Miguel A. Giusti and Amalia Boyer professors of the theme, from one philosophical sight defined the globalization like the increase of the relations maintaining for various groups of the world; the reduction of cultural barriers for interchanging products, ideas or services. The global term hints at the interrelation in different aspects that cannot observe like themes isolated due to technological advances, like the Internet and for political ideologies like the neo-*liberalism* that promotes the commercial interchange.

In an article published in the magazine" Harvard Business Review" the professor Donald N. Sully of London Business School and Martín Escobari consultant of Brazil, they say that the companies of Latin America encounter one or two options: spreading out or being acquired. *For this chapter, it is the base adding personal concepts and complementing with other consulted sources.*

Motives:

1. For better management of the risk; to do business in markets out of the region, avoiding the concentration.

2. For lack of liquidity that removes a lot of capability of maneuver and he hinders the administration.

3. The tall capital costs that make difficult the capability to generate value.

4. The exhaustion of the opportunities of growth of local markets.

5. Survival: is better than the company act globally that to work for a foreign boss.

They refer to a series of obstacles that they call **"the Latin cost"**, namely:

1. Tall tax burden.

2. Scarcity and raising capital cost; they estimate it equivalent to twice the cost of similar companies in other parts of the world.

3. Corruption; the biggest problem.

4. The size of the market that does not permit investing in research and development neither generating a cash flow enough to finance an international expansion, aggravated for the technological disadvantage in some cases.

Besides they allege that Latin American companies have been slower to answer to defiance's and opportunities of the globalization than the European, Japanese and North American; exchange rates are very volatile; The governmental policies are incoherent; he values of inflation and unpredictable interests and the foreign competition is increasing.

However, the far-sighted companies have answered aggressively to these changes. For example EMBRAER of Brazil, manufacturer of airplanes works with French associates; makes part of production at China; perceive capital in London and New York; hire executives originating better company's of the world and establish offices close to clients but big anywhere in the planet using software of last generation, without caring from where he comes. They too mention CEMEX, BUNGE, CVRD, ARCOR, TELMEX and TELECAST like companies that have become global leaders to weigh of obstacles at his respective industries.

I. CRITICAL STEPS

According to them, the companies that have been globalization have taken common steps, that is to say:

1. They are committed with **a global mentality**.

2. The executives undertook daring actions to make their commitment **irreversible**.

3. They realigned the totality of the organization to **compete globally**.

With respect to the step one, the point of view of the company cannot see oneself. The local perspective avoids the world theme; the fact that represents in the portfolio of global investors, clients, suppliers and executives, whose resource needs in order to fend of big corporations; the treaties help to change the local intention; studies out-of-doors, quoting in stock exchange global markets, the good corporate government

An excellent practice consists in identifying the best company of the world in category and to analyze the difference utilizing the benchmarking, in order to know the variables that dial change. The intellectual must have honesty to watch the cool head and humility to acceptance.

With respect to the second step they recommend:

1. **Focalizing:** concentrate on an only business and no committing the imprudence to penetrate into many fields.

2. **Making a bet to check mark** with strong investments in marketing.

3. **Looking for an alliance** even selling communication company.

4. **If it is ringing,** changing home womb and official idiom.

5. **Establishing a loud relation** with a customer keeping to the height of his requirements. The leader must be a partner and besides, tack risk over the race.

6. **becoming stronger in technology** to achieve productivity investing in critical processes.

7. **Making the logistic process perfect**.

As to the third step, requires **vision and a long-term commitment**; proximity a decade become effective and sometimes takes more time. The strategic marks must established direct the expansion; knowing when and where doing acquisitions or alliances; doing obvious processes for aspects critics of transformation; generating solid relations with international capital markets; suppliers and with clients keys and above all, **globalize the executive team** and corporate moral values.

2. BASIC QUESTIONS TO ANSWER

a. ¿Does we have a local base?: if it is, should be strong and generate cash flow enough, that they permit standing losses operating that generally present while to penetrate international markets.

b. Do are they attacking us now? Is very difficult to defense and attack at the same time.

C. It is very later? If right, now the other ones are positioned, it is preferable to go into another type of alternatives.

d. It is local business by nature? Certain types of services and products that are not exportable exist.

e. Does he prefer to be rich or king? "Poor person's king" or "rich without reign" The globalization demands a good corporate orientated government to protect the little shareholders and offering foreign investor's confidence.

f. Does he have stomach to do it? The defeats hurt very much and who the global makes a decision is willing to it.

g. Is he determined to invest in the long run? These processes take long and in some cases to 10 years according to authors.

When all human team talk the globalization must understand that it is seriously. It implies breaking with the past and to impede that go back to incur in the initial situation. Credibility must be instilled, speaking plainly and acting with courage (breaking off habitual way to do business).

Who talk about these themes has to look at the China. After having been the nation but advanced in the century XV (the compass, the printing house, the paper and the most modern maritime fleet of the planet) decided close his frontiers in 1433. At a later time, in 1978 has placed the process of reform initiated by **Deng Xiaoping** on a modern country with gigantic companies again that get the most of the economies of scale and turn into the competitor and threatening for United States. The main character of the century XXI that turned upside down the worldwide equilibrium and, for that reason all countries must try to strengthen his relations with the new stair.

The worldwide Forum (Davos, Switzerland) concluded that nowadays worldly situation is fragile, complex and dangerous; the increasing interconnection among distinct spheres has created a great impact. The economic development is narrowly related to social progress, the free trade, and the good government practices countries; chains united in search of common objectives **of value generation**.

The crisis became dominant level of governments, institutions and companies. An arduous job of government, businessmen and academy to recover the ethics, the moral values and honesty are required. It is fundamental to be able to recover the confidence and advancing toward prosperity.

The poverty (4,000 million in the world) and hunger get constituted in the seed of fanaticism, the intolerance, the violence and chaos. The generate of value, based in legitimacy political that is needed urgently. This does not turn well, if do not distribute the benefits of progress for all.

The worldly poor (if get busy) become an enormous potential for companies with plant capacity idle. The globalization has to become inclusive. The rich countries must give a free entrance to the products of poor countries and require these improving the government, the productivity and social aspect.

The companies must respect all interest groups; the good corporate government becomes imperative; just the same, must assume crucial themes and engaged with communities; equally being made sure not harm the countries where act, preserving the environment and respecting the cultural moral values.

An almost indispensable complement, in terms of globalization, would say certification of The Coalition impresario anti-smuggling, BASC like element of competitiveness, because he reduces the supervisory costs, speeds up the step and makes easy the Metrology

The BASC turns the certainty into a strategic element to develop the external markets, because it is devoted to promoting actions for provisional remedy to avoid the smuggling and drug trafficking making easy the international trade.

In order to complete, the practical importance of international certification in quality, human development, preservation of the environment and BASC are another universal idiom; the steps in international business break of the base of respect to the modern world requirements and very especially, accepting right of satisfaction like customer.

Chapter 8

HOW TO MAKE A COMPETITIVE ENTERPRISE

This chapter had been written on the basis of the book "Less is Further" of Jason Jennings.

The opportunity to find a practical and manual based in real experiences of worldly efficient companies push me to write in simples words for approach the opportunity for learned and to contribute the management development. **Jason Jennings** says than in highly productive companies, culture is the system and a series of systems compose the culture.

Jennings in his book "Less is Further", choose the following enterprise:

1. Ryan air—European Airline

2. Jantech—Manufacturer (U. E.)

3. Ware House—Whorehouse of discounts (New Zealand and Australia).

4. Nucor—Little Steelworks (Half West—U.E.).

5. Ikea—Shop of furniture (Sweden and Denmark).

6. World saving—Financial Institution (U. E.)

7. Yellow Freight—Terrestrial Transport Company (U. E.)

The culture has a base in:

- A set of deeply seated moral values.
- A sequence of work efficiently organized and systematized.
- An environment in which the work is done in accordance with better practices identified by the men in charge to do it.
- A joint desire to eliminate the waste and to reach a level lifted of productivity.
- A competitive environment, which each one of related proceedings serves as starting, point for the continuous improvement.

We must turn essential functions into systems and to accomplish them one time and another time with the **single-minded purpose** to eliminate the waste and to improve every day.

Jennings in the first chapter refers to only **great objective** that suits his purposes like unifying force and presents a great discovery: in productive companies the great objective is the strategy and it becomes culture; all the rest are tactics to achieve it.

All workpeople must know that great objective, clear and simple and made all efforts to get it. The big leaders impede that the effort of productivity be distracted with any fashionable strategy or with management's last theory.

All team must **center the attention**; concentration is the road to be able to act rapidly and thus to improve the efficiency in all the levels and as a result logic, **generating value** in terms of cash flow, maximum financial indicator.

For it, Jennings recommends six tactics:

1. Enjoying the objective, performing all in the same directive.

2. Selling the objective (orientated process to generate culture).

3. Discovering the people arranged to change and making a bet on them.

4. Seeing off a few; the people that are willing to achieve the great objective are the more important resource; we love and appraised them.

5. Quitting whatever that distract the attention of the great objective, because we must concentrate on achievement it.

6. Demonstrating that the commitment is long-term. The outstanding people do not get connected to a great long-term objective if not they assure future to him. While the team's bulk is occupied of the day-to-day routine, **the heads think about the future**.

The standard ISO 9000 version 2000 stresses the customer's satisfaction and the continuous improvement. The customer's level of satisfaction is calculated with a very severe index, the level's product out of courtesy (deliveries on time) and the percentage out of courtesy in bulk, according to the following formula:

$$ISC = \frac{N^\circ \text{ of given orders in time}}{\text{Programmed orders}} \times \frac{\text{given amount}}{\text{asked for amount}}$$

Which must print monthly for all the possible roads of the company in order that be turned in number of collective handling and thermometer of the principal action of improvement.

1. TACTICS

a. **The truth:** "it is not possible to construct a productive company which **confidence** not is one of principal challenges in and that confidence where he does not exist cannot be in to the truth". The people submit to the leadership of other providing that they get that he tells the truth always.

b. **The frankness:** "the lack of frankness gives space inevitably to pieces of gossip and the rumors, which spread out like a forest fire in autumn".

c. **The numbers:**

- "The productive companies drive openly all the numbers and they enroll all of the important".
- "The one and only modus operandi a productive company is when everybody the world the owner thinks as it were".
- "The people need to feel at ease with oneself every day and they get it through triumph".

d. **The communication:** it must be open. "Tactical plans as a mere formality successfully the great objective they do not come of ivory tower; closer people are operations that they plan better tactics".

The workpeople must trust completely his compensation; the suppliers and customer must know that we have **everything the right** to a margin of profit.

e. **The criticism:**

- "The productive companies criticize the processes, not the workers""
- "The worker that generates value, obvious must be appreciated above all".

Independently of management style, all the actions is expressed in measurable terms. Universally takes from the board of command, the result statement, the balance sheet and, very especially, of the cash flow generate by means of **job in team**, each one contributing and being **implacable judge** with who do not his job, because he is acting contrary the maximum directive.

The leaders of the organization have the **ineludible responsibility** to get engaged with this plan and becoming apostles in his natural circles, to create a culture of **courtesy**, continuous improvement and immediate action and **pleasant environment** that allow to the people to work **HAPPY**.

2. DESTROYING BUREAUCRACY AND SIMPLIFYING

For it he recommends eight steps namely:

1. When decide making a change, do it with celerity and decision (shoot).

2. Get the correct people's support that take communion with the great objective and are willing to take possession with enthusiasm. The workers that oppose the great objective must be fired.

3. Destroying the empires and constructing inter-functional equipments. The company must modify particular dominions in order that they act in terms of the general objective.

4. Decentralizing to create enterprising spirit. To bring decisions near to the clients.

5. To flatten the organization for answer sooner to the client's. The boss of productive companies answer pats the clients and workpeople.

6. Creating fervor among rows. Being visible example and to demonstrate the ranks an interest. It must be made proceedings in order that the personnel see with his own eyes how his leader's acting.

7. Creating and reinforcing a culture of tall performance. Use recognition and promotions to the people.

8. Seeing all of the decisions in order to help the customer. Failing that, it is bureaucracy and must be eliminated.

The author is especially strong in the case of executives and managers that do not serve; the incapable to help the organization to reach the objectives.

He opposes emphatically mass layoffs. The productive companies regard the workers as the more valuable assets and if a layoff is need are because the company has not well driven. If keeps and foments the good employed guy's development, evaluating all constantly and getting rid who have not shown good performance, it not be need to do mass layoffs.

Besides with that classroom of layoffs companies:

- Loses valuable knowledge if not are transference of institutional memory.
- The workpeople that remain lose motivation and go into a status of anxiety and pessimism. Save who can it.
- It proves to be costly to dismiss workpeople and after going back to enter another.
- The mass layoffs do not generate productivity neither hold it.

Bring importance to personnel's selection; tries to know if the person inserts within culture, but also that t respecting the moral values and inserting the company.

He recommends contracting out for the labors that are not vital in business, when they are generic and they do not represent competitive advantage.

Employees and executives must be versatile, that implies great knowledge of the organization.

They give agrees on especial cases the indoor work when they give a detailed report and when based in results.

All entrepreneurial decision must respond to a question that they call murderer:

Is it entrepreneurial logic to do this?

The executives must leave the ego, surpassing the need to defend previous decisions and being capable to abandon the policies of the past when they are obsolete. Besides, all the company's personnel must have the ability to make comfortable the system.

They must identify some motors of productivity and beginning to measure in quantities and no in moneys. Use indicators that invite the action; drive with property administrative and operation levels of the organization, in order that not turn history. He knows quickly that right now and with the indicators of steps must confirm the annual accounts.

For the better a process a system must exist. Brent Hendrix, the engineer of the General Motor defines it like:

"A job in sequence of activities organized of efficient manner and than a team repeat time after time".

The objective is to eliminate the waste and to reach an elevated level of productivity; it gets constituted in starting point the continuous improvements.

In a system:

- All workpeople do the processes of the same manner all the times.
- Previously, has identified him the best modus operandi the process.
- Any one must accomplish the task without introducing variation itself.
- The way that the task comes true he becomes the starting point for the continuous improvement.

The systems must be applicable in all the areas of the company's. The management must prepare to confront some resistance, because some will do all that be within reach to rein; other ones believe that they rank above them and do not desire that others they measure his productivity.

Confidence and respect are required in order to implement a system; continuous improvement is based on common sense. The things decide on the basis of the merit of alternatives and no on the basis the hierarchy existent.

The continuous improvement consists of seven steps, namely:

1. The leaders must participate. Going, seeing, and getting involved.
2. There is agreement in the objectives (identified in motors with indicators).
3. To know the true precise the product or service.
4. One must begin elaborate an existent process's map.
5. The people that accomplish the work must get involved with the new process.
6. The improved process is established immediately.
7. The continuous improvement becomes peculiarity of the company.

He refers to the systems of remuneration like grand company's unknowns. Unless engage in company culture, and be easy to understand, generate confusion and dissatisfaction. The interdependence exists in companies; if cause conflicts for individual remuneration can fall in a dysfunctional environment.

"When the people are ease in his work, they do not worry about his remuneration; but when this displeases, worry for money to foreground dried".

"The remuneration for productivity helps identifies if somebody not fit in culture", because they permit:

- Discarding the people that they do not fit well.
- Organizing about groups.
- Fomenting the team spirit.
- Reinforcing constantly the culture.
- Rewarding economically hard and intelligent work.

"When people have appropriate tools and work as a team; have his performance's exact records; feel worthy from being able with his financial destination, the productivity attains unsuspected heights".

Quote the case Nucor, where all the personnel's remuneration is based on the performance. "The weekly check of the hardworking Bile Smith in Nucor's plant depends so that Bile and his team had produced the previous week. The frankness and precision of numbers per hour, per day and per week are crucial in the company; once the executive director was included, he wins of to sane with productivity".

As the present moment with the internet, the same information is available for whole the world because technology has made possible the democratization of knowledge. The competitive advantage is in capability to execute; the productivity depends on activity related to management; the midways to achieve it are to the reach of wholes. Technology does not guarantee the success and we do not have to be slave of the latter development. The more important is to maintain the entire group marching to the same rhythm.

He defines the motivation as the expression:

"doing than a person acted of determined manner."

"When the competition is canalized to the inside an organization toward a goal or external objective, it is possible to create a cooperative culture highly productive. The danger occurs when produce internal wars within the organization; the competition becomes self-destructive, to the organization becomes dysfunctional and finally the system collapses when people begin to retain the information".

The external objective must be discussed openly; the workers can question the leaders and directors but provided it of a respectful manner and layouts of truthful information. The motivation must not be borne in contests, promotions and rewards; must be authentic and for it, the successful companies use three formulate:

a. Create a safe and protected atmosphere:

- Printing felt work, taking care of well-being and the happiness of the works, permitting that they enjoy.
- Converting the workpeople in interested parts and delivering them responsibilities. The sense comes from the selfishness of each employee in his work.
- Permitting that they make mistakes and making of them all university to learn not to repeat them.

- Imposing the teamwork.
- Fomenting the diversity, with people originating of a tall range of sources.

b. Looking for an external enemy, it is opposing view in order used like integration mechanism.

c. Clearing the road, in order that the group acts. A wise leader initiates and fortress a culture more worthy and more important than any person, included he himself. The eleven characteristics of the leader of a productive company namely:

a. **Pay attention to details** but avoid "extinguishing little fires"; do not try to analyze huge amount of information and numerical analysis's by yourself.

b. **Moral fiber strong:** confidence in something that it is built day by day during all the life; he implies abiding his promises; value and honesty.

c. **Simplicity:** from the clothing that they wear even the decoration of his offices; the houses which they live; the vehicles; they become models of virtue and modesty; the ostentation does not fit in her philosophy neither in the style.

d. **Competitiveness**: it defines clearly a model of competitiveness and injects it to his organizations.

e. **Long-term focus** and share it with employees, the suppliers and clients: they prepare to stand the crises.

f. **Disdain for waste:** "the productivity and success do not stem from not spending money, but the art to know like spending it. They set an example of frugality and austerity and they instill them

g. **Workout in leadership:** the leaders see to themselves like teacher. They show enthusiasm to share the moral values and dream whom they work.

h. **Humility:** it considers human beings like everybody else and they do not enrapture themselves.

i. **To refuse bureaucracy:** all that not add value is waste and it is the leader's responsibility to eliminate it.

j. **Belief in the other ones:** solid belief the fact is that people will do the right thing if they treat them well.

k. **Confidence:** "they begin confiding in his people. Almost always they are repaid with the same coin and rarely do they end up disappointed".

3. BOARDS OF DIRECTORS

Summary document Portfolio Marzo12/07

Boards of directors constitute a collegiate body to help to that the company be successful and generate value; backing up with his experience and knowledge; no management. They are responsible for the strategic company long-term vision, in addition to have great legal liability.

In general, to function efficiently among commitment, owe:

1. Establishing the strategy, to approve and doing tracking.

2. Verifying that all members of the organization understand his moral values and behave in concordance with them.

3. Safeguarding ethics, the transparency and the order; indicating the right thing and the incorrect.

4. Demanding an adequate internal control system.

5. Watching the risk management.

6. Acquiring a compromise with professionalism and transparency in the preparation of credible information financiers and with no financial.

7. Labeling the company's principal executives and establishing the processes of succession.

8. Driving the crises and situations that they surpass the administration and affect the fulfillment of objectives.

The members must be person with independence opinion that understands the business with dynamics, panorama and threats. Being person guided to the quest of results that generate value; with financial basic and capable knowledge to communicate that think clearly, speaking a plain language; unless one of members take it like personnel in order that talent and experience, give the consequences that is expected in benefit of the organization.

It is important that belong to various disciplines and with entrepreneurial experience, company knowledge and the sector. Besides with great ethical sense, demanding, rigorous and those, they enforce the mandates. They must not be booked up with suppliers, competitors, and groups of shareholders neither with administration in order that they may express his opinions without fears of a classroom.

Usually the monthly meetings make of four to five hours with material previously supplied by administration for his study; twelve previous hours must use work that he takes care of himself in; must get busy, thought that 70 % of the time in chores of planning and 30 % in themes of the past.

They must have an attractive remuneration that generates commitment and reflect the so significant role and the legal liability (civilians, district attorneys and prisons). An equivalent compensation is accepted to the hours demands that the debit, (including the ones belonging to preparation) for the value hour of the company president.

It is recommended avoiding concentration of information in the management because can generate partial communication to the meeting that would slant decisions for the asymmetry that may show up. Equally, committee's conformation specialized with participation of some member of meeting for specific themes.

Chapter 9

REFLECTIONS ON LEADERSHIP

Many and very recognized authors,[1] have written depth on the leadership; it is a difficult theme; I want to do an approximation combining reading matters whose authors appointment, with my personal experiences.

1. ¿WHO IS A LEADER?

It depends on the reference group; the world has had big leaders that have leaked out like Jesus Christ, Mahomet, Confucius, Mahatma Gandhi, etc. In this case, we are talking of PRODIGY.

The theme is much relative depending of reference groups; a big leader doesn't interest at all. What signifies Juan Pablo II for a Chinese tribe; on the other hand, their cacique, chapmen or how they call him, he is supremely important. The same occurs as we do a political division, for activities, for sports, for sciences, religion, cultures, arts, etc.

All reference groups, with similar characteristics need leaders that contribute to the achievement of the great objective in benefit of the group. The companies required leadership, which can learn to develop directing abilities.

The employee identify with the company and develop his own talent is a determining element for increase the productivity. When people are connected for a salary, begin the true challenge: how achieving that?

The theme becomes complicated because human needs are different; depending of person and because the company needs one high grade of development, to appraise the most important asset which is not owner. It is the work for authentic leaders: ¿ what must do in order that the employees understand and keep in the search of the defined objectives?

The companies cannot buy the humans theirs goodwill, delivery, love for his work, and another one intangible attributes, to discover and to potentiality; is a true defiance for the leader for the position that he occupies. He can increase insofar that live as leader MOTIVATIONAL.

2. THE MOTIVATIONAL LEADERSHIP

According to Bryan Tracy consists in ability to encourage and inspiring other ones in order that t gives the best of them. The personal leadership consists in the ability to **motivate oneself** to get things and to be person's classroom that becomes motivational leader. He is not interested from where you come; the past already happened, but if with the present and if can get modify the future.

In order to develop this capability, the person must have an answer to the question: ¿To where and how am going to arrive? To become an outstanding person, surround, praised, admired and respected must part of the answer. That **makes** the person outside is **been** acts in representation the interior person's.

The person that intends to become **motivational leader** must see oneself like a model to keep an example for others; besides establishing tall standards of responsibility and behavior, reminding that get more easy great part of things in human life by indirect manner.

The power attributed comes due to the interior person (**being**); is a genuine leadership, the more honorable and bigger officer those followers. Confucius talks about servile leadership; he must be the servant.

The present-day leader asks around; listen attentively; glides of diligent manner; to accomplish consent among the elements necessary to get the objectives, beginning to discover the needs of his group to turn on a hope (credible solution).

3. THE LEADER'S ESSENTIAL ATTRIBUTES

VISION: contemplating that perhaps and asking oneself, because no? George Bern Aral Shan.

The motivational leader transforms the people profiting from his hope, dreams and ideals. Should be intelligence to choose the area that permit the team go to accomplish an outstanding job. Besides being excellent in whole that he does; the best in the range of activity that he make.

INTEGRITY: is a complete and unyielding honesty that himself tells relate with everything that does and complete giving the best always; telling and living in the truth.

COURAGE: implies being faithful to beginnings to defend one exercises and not to change opinion, unless convinced about the new alternative. Facing the unknown without guaranteed successful.

REALISM: seeing the things like are and not as we want to see them; no expecting miracles; no believing in luck, no expecting rewards without working; not even the problems put in order themselves (self-deception).

RESPONSIBILITY: is all the opposite to invent excuses, blaming others, getting angry, getting upset or resenting with the other what have done. For lead others is necessary first to be leader oneself.

An excellent person, motivated for a great vision; that advances toward his realization; that inject the enthuses to another for help her; honest with he does; admired and respected; that establishes tall standards behavioral; lives in truth with oneself and with the others; instill confidence; than demonstrates courage for oppose be the circumstances; that knows how to laugh; is realist; refuses lucked games and deceits; capable to assume the responsibility; is ready to **do**, that is the important. **He is a motivational leader**.

A motivational leader is ready to create an environment for the people may accomplish her potential and to achieve the synergy of teamwork, join together, increasing the virtues by the synergy of the summa of individual capabilities.

The investment must facility the conditions for the people may behave like human beings, considering that work is only one of the seven aspects that the individual must drive for a good live(besides must balance the following: relative, religions, economic, health, education, social). Certainly that environment must be translated in an institutional knowledge that constitutes the intellectual capital, which are the more valuable assets in the century XXI, the century of knowledge according to PETER DRUKER. The measurement of intellectual capital in bookkeeping is one defy, in addition to the unification of some universal accounting principles, in concordance with globalization.

Another, very interesting focus of leadership is due to STEPHEN COVEY, who talks about eighth habit. According to his experiences, "people do not fight for the organizations that they work; do not feel realized neither satisfied; do not know where go his institutions and what are his priorities; are depressed and distracted; frustrated and that is worse, they sense that cannot do anything to change the situation".

4. SEVEN HABITS

1. Being proactive.

2. Beginning with the end in the mind.

3. Putting the first thing first.

4. Thinking about winning—winning.

5. Searching first to understand, next know.

6. Synergize.

7. Sharpening the saw—body physical, mental, spiritual renewal.

Define the eighth habit as the quest of own voice, collaborating with others in order that they look for. The voice has only a personal significance that known confronted the highest difficult and makes equals them.

Voice is the attachment that exists among **talent** (natural fortresses), **the passion** (the things themselves naturally give energy, motivate and inspire it), **the need** (including what the world needs to pay to him) and **conscience** (that little voice that tells him that is the right thing and that encourages to do it).

Define the code of the soul as the resulting of: when he acquires a compromise with a job that arouses his talent to and that stimulates his passion that comes from a great need of the world and the voice of his conscience that tells him that must accomplish. Each person maintains a deep, innate and almost inexpressible longing to find them voice of life.

The vision reaches to measure that the person perceives the community's needs and he answers to his conscience treating to satisfy them.

5. THE PAIN—THE PROBLEM—THE SOLUTION

The influence and leadership come from the option, no of the position or the range. We must find our own voice and inspiring the team and the organization to find theirs. Key elements and four correspondent needs:

LIVING, LOVING, TO LEARN AND LETTING A LEGACY

These reflections remind teaching of one to my betters professors (my respect and admiration to all), the S. J. Augusto angel, who in the last days of my professional studies told us: the only thing than bring leadership is the **capacity of help** and I reinforce with another definition according to S.S Juan Pablo II: "a company is a community of persons."

In the book **Less is Further** of Jason Jennings, it is read:

"A wise and fortress leader initiates a culture and after, culture be more worthy and more important than any person, included himself"

Accepting our human condition and thinking about good people, that constitutes a true asset for the company and that maintains a permanent desire of personal growth, implies a lot of reflection and improving required by the leaders:

- Capable to forgive and to get constituted in support for the group gets better.
- That give good deal, thus to announce a layoff.
- They need the practice of empathy that permits give instructions with a look, a facial expression or a sign when the circumstances demand it.

- That they feel happy helping to the other way to potentate his capabilities in addition to his personal growth contributes to the company development.
- That they not forget his human condition and as such invoke SUPERIOR BEING like guide of his purposes that guarantee the goodness of his plans.
- That they maintain to lip flower stimulating phrases like:
  - Let's team up.
  - Let's get in touch.
  - That you hold an opinion.
  - Thanks for your collaboration.
  - I appreciate your effort.
  - How nice.
  - Tranquil that we are going to get better.
  - Congratulations!
- Than among his human condition they be just taking decisions, thinking about all the affected.
- That they be able to maintain the calmness in difficult situation although that the circumstances can be oppose.

6. THE SEVEN "S"

Peter and Waterman refer to variables out of what formal: intuition, the irrational, it informal and they present that they call the seven "S".

a. **Orientation to the consumer:** although to spend time planning and control, priority keeping n touches with the people outside, with a policy of open doors. They management encourage little volunteer's groups to resolve punctual problems.

b. **Proximity to the customer:** developing agile mechanisms to perceive and to resolve the client's problems. The team of sales with specialized technicians gets stronger.

c. **Autonomy and entrepreneurship:** they do not maintain a too strict supervision on people; they promote the overtaking of risks and internal competition heals her. An indispensable practice is innovative in products.

d. **Privileges to the people in the search of bigger productivity:** we all go in the same ship and that does each one the positive print has influence or negatively in the result. The productivity with personal satisfaction is rewarded.

e. **They preserve the moral values and him they spread:** in order to achieve the excellence in the long term, the corporate moral values are the more important variable. The executives of superior level dedicate to maintain the intervening moral values talks long time with the personnel's rest.

f. **Growth on solid bases:** according to authors one never must buy a company, unless he knows, as it must work. The institutions must move one step at a time.

g. **Organizational arrangement** of simple and thin type.

7. FACTORS OF SUCCESS

A. BASICS:

a. **Strategy:** she must clearly know by all.

b. **Discipline and action:** in order to maintain the good habits in the organization.

c. **Structure:** page of paper and flexible.

d. **Moral values and organizational culture:** requires to become more assured, to develop and to hold an entrepreneurial culture of tall performance that he rewards the productivity

SECONDARY:

a. **Talent:** they select highly competent people; privilege the formation of new talent and retain the better.

b. **Invention:** essential characteristic for the century of knowledge and technology.

c. **Leadership**: leader's group that they inspire to the rest of the personnel to identify opportunities and to come ahead to the problems.

d. **Growth and organizational development:** good be like individual action or through mergers, acquisitions and, or alliances.

---

1. See www.theodinstitute.org
2. See www.theodinstitute.org

Chapter 10

MAKING A DECISION CORRECTLY

The specialist in this subject teaches that we have to believe that we see. For make grand developments is required changing over **paradigms**, new form to see the universe.

The world changes to gigantic steps, especially for the advance of technology; we have to begin make specifies changes to compass of times to turn into good executers and to avoid falling in the whirl of mediocrity.

We must learn how convert an idea (creative thought) to the successful result. Peter Drunker say: in the century XX we increased enormously the laborer's productivity; in the century XXI, the defiance consists in incrementing the executive's productivity.

The leadership focused toward the personal growth, the executive that exert influence on the others, must recognize all the moral values of his directed and so, he is be able to increase the human capital, the most important resource entrepreneurial; people mark the difference in this century. The great advance of technology and information socialized of knowledge; we needed the intelligence to utilize it.

The universities and all companies must take care of his human group to teach thinking with logic to power the resource; the works generate productivity;

the organizations must put in how know increasing the profitably and as a consequence his patrimony.

The effort must be guided to **connect** idealism and intuition with logic pragmatism. The companies must implement environments that permit the people live better and enjoy working for increase the productivity. Combination of the intellectual coefficient with **emotional intelligence** for radiates to become a **culture**.

The handling of the information permit **management by exception** and frees time to **think** and for other aspects, because work is only one and permits getting him the indispensable resources to satisfy basic needs, speaking in a pragmatic language. The other ones: relative, social, economic, religious, educational, health, they must drive in balanced form to achieve a complete life.

Take decisions are inherent to administration; all schools of business insist to the exercise and apparently, all graduates know how to do it. In practice, indecision is a level entrepreneurial common factor. In general, people are dubitative to finish off, situation that we fed back with unkind criticism to the person that takes a decision; sometimes, we asked for decisions without giving enough judging elements to do it.

The human group has to learn how to take decisions utilizing all of the available technology beginning for the information that companies must turn into authentic tool, complemented with data bases and the internet, which is to reach all. The true intelligence consists in becoming **adapted** to new technology, and utilizes the information, to extract it useful and to dispose of the unnecessary.

It is required to learn how to develop the **emotional intelligence** to accept the facts, to drive the ambiguity, to participate actively in interdisciplinary groups; forgetting about the important that the person believe to be (no necessarily equal that he is); developing curiosity and capability to investigate and above all, disposition to acceptance serenely the decision that the group take independently of one opinion. When the decision corresponds to the higher level, the executive have to act on its own opinion, because always, someone may say that he is wrong.

The Dr Rose Argentine Rivas of the **Silva of Mental Control** in a lecture dictated in Bogota, Colombia explained that decided is inherent to the life; it is something very normal. A guide to make it right: **decide always looking for his inner peace**.

The movement **Slow Food in Europe** proclaims that people must eat and drinking the foodstuff slowly and with complete conscience of the object; besides recommends going back to take the human essential moral values; enjoy the little and quotidian pleasures and a simple live in order to take easy the common decisions.

To take entrepreneurial decisions, the executives must participate with great facility in interdisciplinary groups, **if have the necessary formation**. To implicate only the people that has the responsibility of decision to avoid the loss of energy. The process must be agile, transparent and without asymmetries[2] in the information.

Must establish clearly **how**, that is, the criteria are gone to apply for finishing off. Some need the decision and others take it. The executive's involucres must solemn commitment depending of the parts: that **need** the decision, contribute with the necessary and clear information specified in broad outlines; that go to take a decision do it independently.

The difficulty to take decisions in companies by factors like: the ego, special interests, unnecessary arrears, unjustified distrust, edicts, the urgency, functional blindness, political or position power; fear and bad preparation that must take it and of the people that need the decision. Besides because every time that a decision is needed, is common to find that a distinct and incoherent process is invented.

The important is that the company must circumscribe a clear mechanism to take decisions like a policy and respect it jealously. Teamwork is basic and the group must be convinced that the take decision is looking for the best opportunity to the company, independently of any particular benefit.

The system is design for equipment of height performance; all members engaged and implicate in the decision, at the end of the process must feels them happy and the team most strong.

GENERAL PROCEDURE

- Elaborating carefully the list of required activities to make a decision.
- Assigning one responsible for each of activities.

- Defining a reasonable and convenient time for each activity with each of the responsible.
- Preparing a matrix called "the blessed womb", in the book **Business Think,** which add a column to control.
- Doing the correspondent tracking.

Example: Let's suppose that he goes to buy a machine for an industrial enterprise's productive process.

Steps	Decision	Who	When	How	Control
Investigation	Pre/selection of suppliers	Executive M	February 28	Advisory group (diverse means)	-
Initial contact	To make specific meeting with interested	Executive M	March 30	Using diverse means	-
Demonstrative meeting	To continue the process or to reject	Executive K	April 15	Conference using diverse means	-
Visit installation	To accept by means of the corrections	Executive L and M	May 30	Direct observation	-
Economic evaluation	To accept ...	Executive R	June 15	Qualitative and quantitative models	-
Physical alternatives	To choose one or two options	Executive S	June 30	Analysis	-
Taking decision	To accept or to reject	Presidency	June 30	Validating the process	-

1. They all must have the same available information
2. the book Business Think[2], present eight basic rules to take a good decision:

a. **Growing away from his ego in the door:** because it is insecurity and arrogance something that each person can control. The humility must be practiced, reminding that in the long run each person is an inhabitant but. Take care of the time and energy.

b. **Generate curiosity:** exploring the unknown flexibility is generated and they turn on minds that appear productive ideas. He must become a corporate value instilled from the maximum hierarchic value.

c. **Draw away from the solution**: do not accept predetermination solutions; if the solution does not generate value for the company nothing is not value.

The money is essential in business; the cash flow is the most important for a company and the projection of cash flow is the fundamental financial tool.

d. **Obtain proof:** on the contrary there is a reason to do nothing. The speed to obtain the proof and to convert it in concrete data for next to accelerate as much as it can must be reduced. A fast and false decision can become a problem. In VOLVO, Swedish company, any project slow two years in materializes, even though the idea is bright and simple.

e. **Calculate the impact:** it consists in quantifying what is not appreciated immediately. Utilize the questions: how does measure it? How much is he? How much should be he? Which is the difference? How long do we need? Checking don't be superior the cost of the compromise to the cost of the problem. GO on the subjective to objective. A prognosis of cash flow must be done.

f. **Explore the effect of wave:** make sure to know be more than enough who else, or be more than enough as the company's another aspect has consequences taking care of the macroeconomic surroundings to end to understand the complete reach of the solution.

g. **Slow down in front of warning signals:** if business is too good why don't have other ones?

h. **Look for the cause:** make sure to treat the cause in place of his effects. For it nothing better than the elementary question why? Why? Why?

---

1. They all must have the same available information
2. Business Think. Dave Marcum; Steve Smith and Mahan Koalas. Page 30.

Chapter 11

THE GENERATION OF VALUE AND THE HUMAN RESOURCE

OG MANDINO, the wise of the sales said in a congress on trade for times of crisis, in Bucaramanga, Colombia: the world is and will continue being unjust; it corresponds to the good men, to do something to change the situation, in benefit of all the humanity.

In the world-wide economic FORUM reunited in Davos (Swiss, 2003) the assistants concluded that the present situation of the world is fragile, complex and dangerous. The crisis of confidence became a dominant factor in the scope of governments, institutions and companies, reason why recommended an arduous work to in equipment with the academy to recover the ethics, the values and very specially, the honesty.

The world must recover the confidence, which is fragile, difficult to establish and easy to break like step fundamental to advance towards the prosperity; the economic development is closely related to the social progress, the free commerce and the good practices of authority. The govern ability is based on the political legitimacy and this one is obtained if the progress is distributed in a balanced form.

A frontal attack against the corruption is required, especially in the called institutions to instill confidence based on its transparency like the educative, churches, police, institutions, the army, the collegiate bodies and in general, of all the people who run some investiture for teach with the example.

Is clearly that for exists bribing, must have a briber, with culpability depending on the interpretation the dilemma that sister raised Juana Ines De la Cruz:" who freckle more, that pays by the freckle or who freckles by the payment? The lack of principles of some leaders, the cult to the easy money in the consumer society and the lassitude of the laws constitute an epidemic to eradicate.

The poor men of world—if they become occupied are an enormous potential for the companies with capacity of idle plant. If no, they constitute themselves in the seed of the fanaticism, the intolerance, the violence and the chaos, factors that attempt against the quality of life of the others.

China finishes giving to a passage in this sense, in the last plan (2006-10) oriented to social justice and the adjustment of the distribution of the entrance, gives the greater importance to reduce the poverty, to increase the unemployment, to improve the conditions of life and for defending environment.

Before the previous dilemma, is urgent that the inclement globalization opens to spaces to the poor people generating opportunities of growth with fairness.

The countries of smaller degree of development require the aid for improving the productivity of developed counties, but opening the doors to its products and offering them to consultant's office and capital in all its forms (intellectual, technology, money, etc).

The companies must respect all the groups of interest and to commit with the communities being preserved environment and respecting the values, to combine the interest deprived with the public well-being being contributed to improve the quality of life because, if the society is not viable, for obvious reasons the businesses are not it either.

According to C.K. Parlad, professor of strategy, university of Michigan, exists a great opportunity and, at the same time, the humanity can made save fortune. The greater potential market of the world is the consumers of smaller resources, which are considered in approximately 5,000 million of person. The positioning in these sectors in order to look some actions for to do.

The entrepreneurs must take an inherent mission, based on their condition of leaders: the generation of work, almost a natural right of all people in terms of social justice. In addition, to execute the transformations necessary to increase the productivity; to make, to prices that these potential consumers can buy. The emergent markets accept quickly new technologies; we must innovate with products that help to solve problems and to learn to enjoy doing it, obtaining profits superior to the capital cost, which in his simpler expression constitutes the concept of **generation of value,** in financial terms.

$$EVA = r - CC$$
It generates value if r > 0

r: patrimonial yield
CC: cost of capital

$$EVACp \text{ (josavere)} = \frac{U + IyD + Po + Cp + Ots}{P + Aj} - CC$$

U: operative utility
IyD: investments in investigation and development
Po: investments in positioning
Cp: investments in the human resource
Ots: other able to be capitalized expenses
P: patrimony
Aj: adjustments to the patrimony (of diverse kind)

That don't measured, don't is, improvement; is necessary to measured with the index of generation of value, independently of the type of organization. The important is to define clearly the appropriate indicators for the company, because badly measure with the same pattern to a company of anonymous investors who to a corporation of social interest or a state company.

The accounting is a technique that is implemented relatively easy. The complex, which truly occupies to us in this occasion, is the exposition of alternatives that allows us to create a culture of **value generation,** which in highest proportion depends on the human resource.

HOW TO MAKE IT POWERFUL

The worker happy and concentrated in which they are doing, that is to say, living the moment; here and now, with an oriented philosophy to satisfy the final consumer. But, the companies are part of surroundings in which the life is very complex in regard to the insecurity and the conflicts that are to each step, in addition, in some cases, of the badly the treatment received for the citizens from the institutions of the state, until paying taxes.

In the Latin American Forum on security and citizen coexistence celebrated in Medellin, Colombia in 2006 reached the conclusion that is a problem of multiple facets and that requires many actions of diverse nature to solve it.

The state must recover spaces that serve as centers of encounter, to create a coexistence atmosphere and to instill in public employees, the elementary norms of respect which deserve the citizens, which as well, would give all the moral authority to demand it. In the same way, the people must assume the conduct that corresponds, beginning by the search **of inner peace**.

It is urgent a plan of shock to reduce the liquor consumption to more moderate levels and to avoid all the negative sequels that it generates; the serious problem for a state barman, especially as far as concerns the local taxes. That to say, of the problems of another type of drugs no controlled by the state.

Chapter of special attention is the intra familiar violence, where the seed of hatred is generated; being the most affected the women and the children.

When we spoke of these subjects is required to think about youth so neglected and with few spaces in some countries that offers very counted opportunities to them, which induces them to take refuge in gangs to find recognition and approval with serious sequels, specially for the familiar atmosphere and serving as negative example the children, who often are direct or indirect victims in other cases.

The sport and the culture constitute excellent mechanisms to attack the problem and to help to improve the quality of life, reason why they deserve to be center of attention of the government as far as concerns regulation and main directorate and to the industrialists like sponsored.

But while this happens, which will take long time because it requires policies of long term and don't constitute object of statues or something similar, the industrialist must begin to develop in the plants centers productive that resist hostile means to that referring to make of its organizations an **pleasant place** so that people enjoy when workings.

Institute THE GREAT PLEASES TO WORK publishes a roster of the best companies to work in the world, which we could call companies "sky" which will be able to be given the luxury to choose the best collaborators in regard to its good reputation, which will as well increase its potential of generation of value.

The institute affirms to know clearly evidences that demonstrate a direct correlation between the best places to work and their results in terms of **generation** of **value**; It measure the confidence in the administration with base in the credibility, the respect and the impartiality; the feelings of the employees, based on the pride to belong and the camaraderie.

The good company complements which intrepid actions as the participation in the drive of administration, with salary of risk depending of results, the representation in the boards of directors, the good associate government, and the valuation of the intellectual capital and first of all, a human approach.

Logically we must start off of a person with much human quality, acquires from the maternal belly and developed in its entire splendor in the first eight years of life as in many scenes repeated Dn Reynaldo Arroyave Lopera. We are speaking of responsible paternity and maternity, which correspond more to the conscience that to legislation.

In businesses, is very important discovering objectively, with high degree of certainty the qualities of the personnel to contract and it must constitute the **first preoccupation** of the entrepreneurs, if is going to share with somebody, almost in conditions of partner, it must be very sure.

We have talked about before and that according to the Ethos, institute of Brazil dedicated to help the companies to improve its places of work, in twenty years of investigation, reached the conclusion that the **confidence** between heads and **collaborator** is the basic characteristic that defines the best companies, like site to be used.

Logically, the personal quality must be complemented with the competitions that the position requires for which the person and whose will have to be budgeted in a maximum time of entailment, agreed with the hierarchic classification and its requirements to avoid stagnations that become brake for the development of the company.

The companies cannot have people occupying a position of low profile during an excessively long period of time because they become suffered or an indirect labor cost when finishing the work contract. Person who does not have a development potential, is a problem for the company.

The academy must be reoriented to become jumbled other people's in the practical field and prepare professionals who know the challenges in the know society, their professors understand the enterprise world as Warren G. Venís and James O'Toole talking about to the United States universities. The companies, must open well spaces to the students so that they can make his practices and, to clear the process.

It is important insisted on a holistic approach in the administration education to watch the company like a community of people (Juan Pablo II) in the search of a general benefit that by all means must include social investment, because the private interest must be convergent with the communal property.

The strategic thought is fundamental in the formation of the executives and the academy already begins to prioritize in the development of abilities and skills like the foreign capacity of negotiation and adaptation, leadership, languages, the conformation of value chains and the logistics with programs specially developed for the circumstances of a company, but with a global vision.

After a serious process of selection it must be complemented with a good training initiating by the vision, the institutional mission and values complementing with the specific knowledge of the position. The periodic evaluation as tool of improvement of the performance level and component of the basic wage; the opportunities of personal growth and the good treatment conform surroundings for the happiness, the natural state of a mind heals and constitute the departure point for the **generation of value**. All the others are susceptible to improve in the measurement that the companies have leaders inspired as it must be, based on service.

CHAPTER 12

BUDGETS, SIMPLE NORMS AND CONTINUOUS IMPROVEMENT

A good system of costs[1] must serve like element as planning facilitating the processes as simulation, beginning by the earnings statement projected. To be "good" it must:

- That is appropriate for the particular case (it does not have sense to use ABC costs for an industrial company because they do not take care of the plant capacity).
- That it is clear and easy to understand for the users, especially for those who control it.
- That presents opportune information.
- That it allows applying the administration by exception that induces to us to occupy of the abnormal situations.
- That it indicates clearly the variations negative so that they do not become cost hidden.
- In the case of industrial companies, it must relate the production costs to the capacity budgeted in agreement with the plan of value generation[2].

In agreement with the strategies and the tactics to implement them, aiming at an objective of generation of value we can assign the resources that in countable terms will be costs or expenses and must leave the sales to obtain an specifies of profit, that satisfies the expectations of the shareholders and in which take shape all the activities to develop.

Benjamín Zander[3], director of the Philharmonic Orchestra of Boston attributes his success to the optimism of his preparation to the life and says that the leadership consists of forming you lead that accompany. The optimism must accompany by passion and method. "passion without method is the chaos, and method if passion is the death", wise words that we must consider when we began to work with the tool which we called the *Plan of Generation of Value*, different from the budgets that must serve as guide the centers of responsibility to contribute to the general mission of the company and to which, obvious, all must be subordinates.

When the companies initiate the learning of the planning systems, disciplines that are acquired with the repetitive and analytical exercise, and are perfected with the feedback that becomes through pursuit, require time (costs) that serves as base to initiate the exercise.

A good estimation of the cost is essential and high-priority to elaborate the budgets and these, as well, they constitute a good base to consider the costs and of fixing sale prices that facilitate the sensitivity analysis to us until finding the map course which we must follow to obtain the objective. Of course it is the necessary to made good budgets.

Tad Leahy published a document titled "the traps of the budgeting." that reproduced the magazine MANAGEMENT in which it writes on the indirect effect of a bad budget done. I have taken it as it bases to indicate aspects of improvement in the elaboration of the budgets. **He writes on which he is not due to do**, I say, to my way, **which is due to do**.

1. HOW MUST BECOME A BUDGET

a. **To define the strategic plan**: to design the strategies and to prepare the tactics for its implementation; thus can assign the resources.

b. **Using the suitable information of costs,** rejecting all the correctable errors (cannot consecrate inefficiency). Must purify the information before using it and first of all, to measure the measurable and to think about the relation cost—benefit.

c. **To give active participation to the people** in charge to facilitate that the managers become jumbled him; they take control of the objectives and assume the responsibility to execute them with the suitable expenses.

d. **Not to take them like unavoidable;** if the circumstances change and the generation of value is affected; it is due to reframe to look for the strategic target. The remuneration of the managers and executives must be based on the performance evaluations and on the numbers of sales.

e. **To give it strategic nature**: the macroeconomic conditions and the variables used for their elaboration can be altered by some circumstances. If it happens, must revalue the numbers.

f. **To use suitable software, which can facilitate the standardization of the information**: is due to obtain one simple, with an analytical application for the particular case. It must be appropriate and we must learn to use it.

g. **It does not have to be confused with the business plan,** which must be realistic to combine risks and opportunities. The budget can be used like motivator element and factor of evaluation.

h. **To analyze the deviations judiciously:** the important thing is that somebody takes care to investigate because and suggests a remedial action.

i. **Corporative culture**: like in general, the budgets, of some form imply the concept of "measurement" and to the executives they do not like that "measure them", is very common to find great obstacles in the first stages when the implementation of this discipline begins. It is difficult to take a step of outpost without direct intervention of the president of the organization who, in the measurement that this convincing of its kindness, can impel it openly.

2. STRATEGIES[4]

A good guide to implement the strategy to follow consists of carefully analyzing the matrix of margins of contribution and participation by lines, to see as the average margin can be improved.

The strategy must become a set of simple rules[5].

KATHLEEN M. EISENHARDT AND DONAL N. SULL, professors of the University of Stanford and Harvard Business School respectively, in his articulate "the importance of the simple rules" present five great categories:

A. HOW TO DO: are oriented to organize to the executives in the search of opportunities, examples:

- To use the telephone directory of each city.
- To complement with the use motors of search in Internet.
- To make specific appointments using the email.

B. RULES LIMIT: they serve to select quickly in the middle of multiple opportunities, examples:

- Our potential client must display financial statements.
- We do not take care of countries of Africa.
- We do not take care of orders of 2,000 meters.

C. PRIORITY RULES: they help to define an order for allocation of resources, examples:

- Initially we will take care of the companies located in the five great capitals.
- Its interest to us plus manufacture products.
- Preferential use terrestrial transports terrestrial.

D. OF SYNCHRONIZATION: its help to connect the opportunities by means of a coordination of the different areas from the company, examples:

- Investigation and development must elaborate a chronogram of launching of new products involving to those who must be committed.

E. OF EXIT: its help to discard passed opportunities, example:

- If during three years consecutive did not fulfill certain goals with a particular product retired of ours portfolio.

So that one regulates is simple does not have to be:

A. ample: "we encouraged the qualification of our personnel".

B. vague: "don't sell bad clients to payer".

C. absurd: "to sell solely clients who pruned to control".

D. it expires: "our clients are small industrialists".

The rules often arise from the experience and from the errors. All almost is in head of the personnel; lack to turn them institutional knowledge properly formalized.

All the simple actions of budgeting and norms must orient us to the universal pattern consecrated in 9000 norm ISO version 2.000: "The continuous improvement".

The processes, in addition to the PHVA (to glide, to do, to verify and to act), must have an objective and an action of improvement.

TO GLIDE: while greater is the proportion of time dedicated to a judicious planning, less taking doing like effect of the greater productivity than can be obtained. Our culture this very oriented when doing and despises the planning; almost that we condemned a person if it is being documented or it been thinking. "One goes doing nothing".

That form to act kind against the good execution and in fact affects the quality with the countable complicity that practically ignores the hidden costs or of no quality which would have to be like negative variations that affect the financial results, in last instance, the true measure of the generation of value in the measurement that the assets rent more than the capital cost (with an objective measurement that considers the expenses able to be capitalized). EVAC.

TO DO: the planning takes a suitable method to us that reduces the run time and guarantees to fulfill the maximum objective in trade terms: the satisfaction of the client receiving opportunely the amount that it asked for with the specifications that requested.

To reduce the run time is equivalent to lower costs of manual labor, indirect costs of manufacture, to trim times of delivery and to accelerate the recovery of the costs and the profit of the order. Let us remember an axiomatic principle in finances: "money cost in function of the time".

To produce implies knowledge; it is the result of the selection, qualification, attitude, dedication and level of motivation of the worker that execute processes. Remember the great importance we must give the human resource trying personal growth and improving quality of life, teaching to live the moment;

the concentration to work and to obtain efficiency (effectiveness[6] with quality and generation of value).

TO VERIFY: it implies measurement. In the life we must measure all the measurable and in the companies too. These measurements must periodically register as it demonstrates verifiable of the action of continuous improvement, via productivity. It must be done using the Benchmarking or comparison with the companies of the world, basic tool to face the globalization.

TO ACT: the term makes relation to all the pertinent activities to learn of the error and to perfect the productive processes, including the administrative personnel. In this case, is the great difficulty practical to measure objectifying efficiency? For that reason it is urgent, periodically to make evaluations of performance of the executive personnel and office. In the production plant it is easier to quantify.

In order to clear all the plan of management of the quality, the company must implement the commando[7] board where the strategic plan takes shape in indicators that it served departure the elaboration as the budgets, the design of the simple norms, the plan of pursuit and the remedial actions.

Finally, it must disclose with all amplitude, involving all the people, to his measurement, and complement with a policy of salary of risk, respecting basic ones that allow a worthy life in agreement with the position that development. ■

---

1. See *Manage mental Costs*
2. To Generate Value: All activity that we do and that the client this arranging to pay by her.
3.
4. He consists of defining an objective and identifying the assets and the actions to obtain it.
5. The strategy of simple rules emphasizes in the processes nails and develops a pattern that gives form them (they serve as guide).
6. Effectiveness: to fulfill the objective without generating value.
7. See *Strategic Finances*

www.ingramcontent.com/pod-product-compliance
Lightning Source LLC
Chambersburg PA
CBHW030913180526
45163CB00004B/1810